Charles Wentworth Dilke

The British Empire

Charles Wentworth Dilke

The British Empire

ISBN/EAN: 9783337165345

Printed in Europe, USA, Canada, Australia, Japan

Cover: Foto ©ninafisch / pixelio.de

More available books at **www.hansebooks.com**

OPINIONS OF THE PRESS

ON

THE BRITISH EMPIRE

"Sir Charles Dilke's new book is assured of world-wide attention, and it is mild commendation to say that it should run through many editions. . . . It will certainly take its place at once as the book for average men on the Queen's dominions. The whole forms a worthy companion to the author's earlier but not more instructive volumes. It is an invaluable contribution to the literature of Imperialism."—CRITIC.

"A useful and eminently readable little book."—DAILY TELEGRAPH.

"In balance and proportion and general conception, this little volume is an ideal text-book, and it is written in a style which makes it not only instructive but agreeable."—ECHO.

"Contains a good deal of information in small bulk, and may be commended to those who wish to study the Empire of which they are citizens."—SCOTSMAN.

"A faithful portrait. . . . Sir Charles Dilke's strength is his power of seeing the facts, a power in which he is absolutely without a rival."—MORNING POST.

"It is really quite astonishing with what ease Sir Charles has got such a vast subject into such a small space, and made so many striking points about the whole and most of the parts."—PALL MALL GAZETTE.

"A most valuable and instructive little book."—LITERARY WORLD.

"The volume seems to us the ideal of what a book on Imperial politics ought to be."—LEEDS MERCURY.

"We have read no better, no clearer account of the multifarious energies of our race than this. . . . Just the sort of book good citizens want to read."—GLASGOW HERALD.

"Admirable. . . . Sir Charles Dilke writes with a fulness of knowledge and an experience of affairs such as fall to few men, and he writes so weightily that his hastiest sentences must give us pause."—OUTLOOK.

a

THE BRITISH EMPIRE

THE
BRITISH EMPIRE

BY

THE RIGHT HON.
SIR CHARLES W. DILKE, BART., M.P.

AUTHOR OF
"GREATER BRITAIN," "PROBLEMS OF GREATER BRITAIN," ETC.

A NEW EDITION

LONDON
CHATTO & WINDUS
1899

THIS VOLUME IS A REPRINT OF A SERIES OF ARTICLES
CONTRIBUTED TO SEVERAL NEWSPAPERS
DURING 1898

CONTENTS

CHAPTER		PAGE
I.	A Bird's-Eye View	1
II.	India	14
III.	The Dominion	33
IV.	Newfoundland and France	46
V.	The Commonwealth of Australia	69
VI.	New Zealand	86
VII.	Africa	100
VIII.	Crown Colonies	113
IX.	Imperial Defence	127
X.	Conclusion	135
XI.	How to Study the Empire	145
	St. Pierre and Miquelon: a Note	152
	Index	153

THE BRITISH EMPIRE

CHAPTER I

A BIRD'S-EYE VIEW

THE British Empire, with its recent extensions in the form of protectorates and spheres of influence, has an area of nearly four Europes, public revenues of 260 millions sterling (without counting the vast sums raised in the United Kingdom by local rates), a population of 400 millions, and half the sea-borne trade of the world. It stands at the top of almost every scale by which Powers are estimated, except indeed as regards its military strength in land forces: the total war strength of the British Empire, apart from armed police, being almost exactly the same as the peace footing of the

Russian Empire, namely, 950,000 men. The British Empire produces almost every requirement of man, and stands first among the Powers in wheat, wool, timber, tea (as far as value goes—having displaced China), coal and iron (in both of which the United States run us close), and, perhaps now, gold. The doubt as to gold may come as a surprise to some. Our gold-fields in Australia, New Zealand, South Africa, Canada, India, and some of our smaller colonies, are so well advertised that it is a little startling to find that the United States, who do not talk much about their gold in present times, still produce almost as much as we do in our whole Empire, the Transvaal running neck and neck with both, and that Russia produces half as much. Not only is there a close race as regards iron between ourselves and the United States, but in steel they have now beaten us out of the field. In silver we are nowhere as compared with the United States. In precious stones, and most of the minerals besides

A BIRD'S-EYE VIEW

those which I have named, we stand first. In tobacco we stand second to Spain, and in coffee, sugar, and other articles very high. With regard to sugar, the wails of the West Indian planters have made many think that our sugar industry has been destroyed by the bounties of the Protectionist Powers; but, whilst West Indian sugar has been pining, British sugar raised in Fiji, in Queensland, and in some other colonies, has been increasing fast in bulk, and there is not that falling off in total production which might be expected, to judge from the complaints.

The colonizing mania which has seized on Germany and France, and had seized on the Italians, who have recovered after a bad fit, cannot confer on France and Germany an empire similar to our own, because the best places were already in British hands. German colonization has, up to the present time, been singularly unsuccessful; French colonization has at great cost added an enormous African territory to the dominions of the French Republic, but one which is unlikely to yield a fair return upon the efforts which it has involved. The only country which possesses a domain which can be compared with our own is Russia, who not only has an enormous amount of agricultural and mineral resource in her Asiatic territory, but has the immense advantage over us of possessing that territory in a contiguous form, and being practically impregnable and almost unassailable by her enemies. The position which we should hold, had we, as we ought to have, a fleet absolutely supreme against every possible combination, belongs to Russia without the expenditure of money upon ships. She could not be vitally damaged even if her army were far smaller than it is, and as matters stand she could hardly be hurt at all.

The immense wealth of the United States, and the energy of her people, make her a more formidable rival than mere extent of territory would imply, for in extent of territory the Great Republic is but equal to Canada or to Australia. Of Canada, a large

A BIRD'S-EYE VIEW

part is subject to a heavy winter, or is actually barren. On the other hand, the Dominion possesses not only the vast agricultural resources which are known, but mineral resources which we know as yet but little, and which may possibly be found to rival those of the United States. The American Union may in time come to exert a leadership over the whole of Central and South America, and in this way may bring within her orbit a much larger territory, and resources infinitely greater than her own; but there is a good deal of resistance, and her supremacy in the Americas, although probable, may lie a long way ahead. The development of Russia, though rapid, is not likely to be more rapid than our own. But that Germany and France can continue to go the pace of the other Powers is hardly to be supposed, while no other country is worth naming in the comparison.

The influence of our laws and race in the future of the world are beyond dispute. They are continued even by the rival Power of the United States. Whatever might happen to the fabric of the British Empire, Australasia could not be destroyed; and the position of Australia and New Zealand in the southern hemisphere and in the Pacific, must colour the future of half the world.

The British Empire outside the United Kingdom of which I have to write consists, of course, of the Indian Empire, of the eleven self-governing colonies, and of the Crown colonies, and in addition to these, of many protectorates and spheres of influence, some of which are under the control of the Foreign, some of the Colonial, and some of the India offices. Their strange and divergent forms of government I shall contrast in the next chapter. It is not easy to form any estimate of the cost to us of our empire across the seas. Many of the stations, such as Gibraltar and Malta, are held for military reasons, and can hardly be looked upon in any light except as being on the same footing as our fleets. With regard to many of our coaling stations, it is difficult

A BIRD'S-EYE VIEW

to allot the military expenditure which belongs to them as portions of the Empire and that which is expended because they are necessary to the protection of our seaborne trade, which trade might exist and flourish even if we had no dependencies across the seas. So too with the cost of the French and German colonies; it is not easy to say what it is. Algeria is in some degree governed as though it were a part of France itself, and military expenditure in Algeria, which is very great, cannot be separated from the expenditure on the French land forces at home, because the army corps which in time of peace is stationed in Algeria, is utilized in Europe in time of war, and its place taken by territorial levies, supposing that the sea communications of France with Algeria are not cut, as they might be cut by a British fleet. The French expenditure upon colonies is on a much higher scale than our own, and money has been poured forth like water by France in the French Soudan or back-country of

Senegal. It has been computed that the French colonies cost over two millions sterling, in addition to the expenditure from the Estimates of the War Office and from naval votes. The German colonies, which are mainly new and chiefly African, also cost a large sum of money for very intangible results. The German trade with the German colonies is very small, and the German civil population in German colonies almost non-existent.

No country possesses a dominion which in the least resembles India, and a comparison with the Russian Caucasus and Turkestan, taken together, would more fit the case of India than any comparison with the colonies or dependencies of any European nation.

The moral to be drawn from the circumstances which have been described, is that the growth in the popular mind of the ideal of what, in his admirable " History of British Colonial Policy," Mr. Hugh Egerton calls "a world-empire, sea-girt, and resting on the command of the sea," forms, as he says, an answer to the "recrudescence of militarism amongst the Continental Powers."

To the marvellous Empire, of which I have named the leading statistical facts, the name of Greater Britain is now often given, although in common use it is applied only to that Empire with the deduction of the United Kingdom. When I first used the term in writing, in 1866-67, the book which I published under that title in 1868, I included under Greater Britain the countries inhabited by our race, and having our speech and our common law, which are under a different political flag. Popular usage is, however, too strong to give any support to a possible attempt to use the term Greater Britain, as I first used it, for the countries of English speech and English law in addition to those of British rule; and, as Mr. Egerton says of the British Empire, "Perhaps the words 'Greater Britain' best describe the new point of view. A world-empire, the separate parts of which are being more and more closely linked by the discoveries of science, enjoying in each separate part absolute independence, connected not by coercion or paper bulwarks but by common origin and sympathies, by a common loyalty and patriotism, and by common efforts after common purposes, such, amidst much to alarm and to disturb, is the apparent outcome of history, the colonial policy with which Great Britain will enter upon the untrodden paths of a new century." The phrase "Greater Britain," if it is not thoroughly clear to us at home, is still less understood abroad. Those who profess to understand it in foreign countries find it exasperating, and those who are called upon to translate it into a foreign tongue meet with difficulty. Last winter, for example, the *Figaro* rendered the phrase into French and back again by way of making it clear: "La Plus Grande Bretagne —The Highest Britannia."

The question how far this strange Empire, of which we find ourselves more or less in possession by a process of historical accretion, can be more closely knit together, is one which has not unnaturally occupied the best minds of the country. The better the impulse and the more poetic the soul of the statesman concerned, the more likely he is to conceive a close union, not only as desirable, but possible. The more he knows the component parts of the Empire, and especially India, on the one hand, and the great self-governing colonies of Australia, on the other, the more inclined he is to doubt the feasibility of a nearer connection, unless it be merely one for purposes of defence. Proposals for a political union, legislative or even administrative, have recently declined in favour, and were for a time replaced by plans for a customs union, which themselves seem to have seen their best days, and which we shall discuss in the conclusion.

The closer union of the Empire for the purposes of defence is well within view, and war would rapidly bring it into shape.

THE BRITISH EMPIRE

Why, however, it may be asked, should we wait for that calamity, to take steps which all concerned admit would be taken then? Not only are our military forces unorganized as regards any close connection between the forces of the self-governing colonies, of the home country, and of India, but even in the territories which are administered from home there is an increasing want of unity of action. The Foreign Office for some time has had its armies in British East Africa, in Uganda, and in the Central Africa Protectorate. The Colonial Office has long had some military forces of its own, not under War Office command, and has this year greatly increased them by the creation of the West Africa Frontier Force. Surely the time has come for welding these armies, the Indian army and the armies of the self-governing colonies, into one great force, so far as general direction goes. As for fleets, the Australian colonies contribute towards a local squadron which, however, the Admiralty is not allowed to move upon

A BIRD'S-EYE VIEW

intelligible principles of maritime strategy. The Cape has recently offered to contribute an ironclad ship without restriction, and the only counter-proposal in South Africa, which has been made by the Dutch leader, Mr. Hofmeyr, is itself a proposal for large assistance towards a most pressing matter of Imperial defence—a British cable to the Cape, instead of the present detached cables which, all of them, touch foreign ground.

In the next article I shall treat of the Indian Empire; and shall contrast with its autocratic forms the strangely divergent systems of government which flourish in other parts of the Queen's dominions.

CHAPTER II

INDIA

WHEN we come to deal with the Empire in detail, that kingdom within a kingdom—British India—first demands attention. The Queen reigns in the United Kingdom as Queen of England, of Scotland, and of Ireland—three crowns which she unites with her original or older crown of Normandy, represented by the Channel Islands. In the rest of the Empire, outside of the United Kingdom and of India, she reigns as "of the United Kingdom Queen . . . Empress of India." In India she reigns as Empress by statute, and has obtained in her lifetime a separate crown which more than represents the nominal power of the Moguls at the height of their Imperial fame.

INDIA

From the point of view of modes of government, it is not easy to classify the countries within the dominions of the Queen. India is a statutory monarchy, locally autocratic, under legislative securities imposed by the Act of a non-Indian Parliament. But, in practice, the powers of the Indian statutory legislature, which is a non-elective body, are controlled by the Secretary of State (who is himself the creature of our cabinet system), and in the last resort by the House of Commons. The great self-governing colonies enjoy Home Rule, with local cabinets. The Crown colonies, such as those of the West India Islands, Ceylon, and Mauritius, have various forms of government, all of them under the control of the Colonial Secretary, and therefore, also, in the last resort, of the Home Parliament. But Fiji, which is one of them, is included within the Federal Council of Australasia—at present a dormant institution, though it had for a time a fairly useful existence. Some Crown colonies in South Africa are indirectly connected with the self-governing colony of the Cape of Good Hope, through the fact that the Governor of the Cape is also High Commissioner for them, and can hardly dissociate his acts with regard to them from the policy which he pursues under the advice of the Cape Ministers responsible to the Cape Parliament. The protectorates, spheres of influence under chartered companies, and other spheres of influence are also not easily reckoned as a whole in any group, because some of them are indirectly connected with the self-governing Cape Colony, some of them under the Foreign Office, some under the Colonial Office, and some of them under the Government of India. Aden, often supposed to be a Crown colony, is in fact, by statute, a portion of the Indian Presidency of Bombay. Several protectorates in the neighbourhood, including British Somaliland, are under Aden. One island among the British possessions, Ascension, defies

INDIA

all classification, for it is under the Admiralty, and is practically counted as a ship. Cyprus, though under the Colonial Office, is nominally a portion of the Turkish Empire, of which the "integrity" was preserved by a lease. The Crown colony of Hong Kong had, for a while, on the neighbouring mainland a lease from China—now ended by absorption; and the curious doctrine of lease—recently, in the case of Germany and Russia, supposed by some persons to have been novel—was also recognized in the case of Quetta and of the Bolan Pass, and is still recognized, not only in the cases I have named and others, but in the recent treaty with China with regard to territory on the frontier of Burma.

In all this strange catalogue I have placed India first. However extraordinary may be the progress, however marvellous the future, either of Australasia or of Canada, India ought always to be first in our minds when we are thinking of Greater Britain. Not only are her sacrifices for the Empire, as well as the numbers of her population, overwhelmingly the greatest, but, while ten out of the eleven self-governing colonies can take good care of themselves, and cannot be greatly harmed or benefited by anything we may say or do, the contrary is the case with India. India is virtually ruled by the electorate of the United Kingdom, and will continue to be so—the Parliamentary system being inapplicable, even in the opinion of the most advanced Radicals, to such a congeries of peoples, so different among themselves in their stages of civilization, so separated by lingual and racial divisions, so hostile to one another in their creeds. The glory which we may reap from the good government of India is the greatest that we can hope for, and our responsibility towards her people is the highest that we can recognize.

As we are told in the last annual official statement with regard to India, which is that for the year 1896–97, distributed to the House of Commons in August, 1898—unusually late,

INDIA

India has been visited by heavy calamities in the shape not only of war, pestilence, and famine, but in the additional form of a destructive earthquake. The war upon the north-west frontier—the most serious which British India has had to face— is now over, the famine has again been conquered, but the plague is still raging in some parts of India, and causing not only much loss of life, but also much disturbance of trade. The reassuring statements made, in connection with the Budget, by the Indian Minister of Finance, will not bear, perhaps, very close examination, as India borrows even in time of peace. But, nevertheless, the condition of India is less alarming than might be expected under the circumstances of the case.

It is finance which lies at the base of every difficulty connected with our Indian Empire. India, to a stay-at-home Englishman, appears to have a large army. When we consider the numbers of her population, she has one of the smallest armies in

THE BRITISH EMPIRE

the world. Among her native troops the number of white officers is confessedly too small. The use of the army in serious war is impossible, unless a certain number of white soldiers are combined with the native force. But such is the costliness of white troops to India upon our present military system, which was adopted against the wish of the Government of India, and which is a system not thoroughly suited to her needs, that it has been found impossible to increase the white army in India since the increase which was effected by Lord Randolph Churchill. A nominal addition to the Indian army has been made by encouraging the native states to set up what are called Imperial Service Troops. It would, perhaps, have been better to have gradually put down the armies of the native states, which are rather a source of danger than of strength, and to have accompanied that gradual suppression by an increased measure of self-government in matters less important.

The feudatory states of India differ greatly

among themselves. One, the State of Mysore, possesses representative institutions and a kind of Parliament. Some of them are autocracies of a mediæval type. The diversity which exists among them, and the comparative popularity of their rule, in spite in some cases of misgovernment, go to confirm the view—that our own government is too inelastic, too much inclined to treat all parts of India as if they were practically one country, although any unity which exists in India is the mere creature of our rule. There is no matter connected with the government of India which is more interesting than this one of the diversity of the native states, of the uniformity of our rule, and of the popularity of most of the native states as evinced by the choice of residence by those who, living in the neighbourhood of the borders, can adopt their rule or ours at will. Few men, except members of the Indian Civil Service, whose interest or whose class feeling is against a change, have the knowledge which enables them to discuss this question and throw light upon it; but it is an interesting fact that two distinguished members of the Indian Civil Service, who have written upon the matter in recent years, have both admitted that there is an immense deal to be said in favour of native states. My own opinion has always been that, provided we keep the defence of India in our hands, and keep a general control of her taxation for defence purposes and to prevent the growth of customs barriers, there is, on the whole, more to be said for encouraging what may be called native states of very varying types, than for encouraging the growth of centralization under our direct rule. Since the mutiny, the Queen's proclamation, and the taking over of the government from the East India Company, things have virtually remained *in statu quo* as regards these largest questions. We have continued to centralize a little, adopting for the whole of India, for example, an excellent code of laws, and we have introduced a representative

INDIA

element in a slight degree to Provincial Councils, and created municipalities. On the other hand, we have stereotyped the existing native states of 1858 with little change. The countries which, like the Punjab, had after their annexation been treated as distinct, and governed on a more rough-and-ready system than the rest of India, have gradually and perhaps mistakenly been brought under the general system. Now there is one terrible drawback to direct British rule in India, which is admitted by fair-minded members of the Civil Service and even by the Government. The finance of India, just as it does not allow us to keep up a sufficient number of white officers to meet the strain of war, also does not permit the existence in India of a sufficient number of civilian administrators to really govern the country as magistrates, as tax collectors, and as ordinary rulers. The judicial and administrative functions are confused, and they are exercised in districts which are far too vast for individual supervision. The government comes home to the rural cultivator—and it must be remembered that the overwhelming majority of the people of India are unlearned, quiet villagers of a too submissive Oriental type—in the form of the native policeman, employed, for financial reasons, at low wage. The Government have often themselves pointed out that, in Asia—where perjury is a deeply rooted institution—the getting up of all cases by such a police is full of possibilities of abuse, of which the grave scandals which occur from time to time reveal the fringe. This disastrous condition of affairs is unfortunately inseparable from our direct rule under existing conditions of finance; and I confess that the remedy appears to me to be to content ourselves with looking after the general taxation, the defence, and the main lines of communication, and leaving the congeries of countries—some great and some very small, of which India is composed—in a large degree, in internal matters, to rule themselves. Of course, any change in this direction could but be gradual—experimental indeed at first; and it may be said that such an experiment has already been made and has succeeded, where, as for instance in the case of Mysore, we have handed back to native rule countries which, during long minorities, had been in our charge and to some extent subject to our system.

One tremendous difficulty is alleged as standing in the way of any such change as that which I recommend. It lies in the fierce religious feuds, especially between Mahommedan and Hindoo, which prevail in some parts of the country. Great towns, however, where they chiefly rage, would not be left without some garrison. Parts of the country peculiarly subject to such feuds would have to be excepted or to be watched, and the paramount Power would always, with her command of the railway system, and her garrisons at strategic points, have troops to be sent into a disturbed district as they are sent now.

THE BRITISH EMPIRE

The most experienced civilians are conscious of the enormous differences between district and district of India. In a large part of the country, our Government fails to receive the firm support of what is best among the natives, on account of its inability to give sufficient weight to the hereditary and the aristocratic principle, while in other parts, as it has been said, "our weakness is that our Government is unable to be sufficiently friendly to some established system of State religion." The Ameer of Afghanistan is not to our western eyes an enlightened ruler, but, strange though it may seem to us, the Ameer of Afghanistan is, on the whole, perhaps a more popular ruler than an impartial but somewhat cold British Commissioner of the most modern type. While the greater part of India looks with most affection, as well as awe, to a government which strikes its imagination, and of which the proceedings are intelligible to the people, because of the high birth of the ruler and of his recognized position, there are other parts, such as the Presidency towns, in which we have to deal with an educated democracy trained in British ideas, often possessing a considerable mastery of our tongue, and which is fairly represented by the proceedings of the National Congress. This much-abused body does not ask for Parliamentary government for India, and its leading members would be content if, in some portions of the country, municipalities were more free to run without leading-strings, than is altogether acceptable to our civilians. If we were able to thoroughly develop our own system, excellent as a system, provided its expense would allow it to be so worked that its intention should be carried into effect, there would be no more to be said. There can be no better government desired for an Oriental world such as India, inhabited by a vast number of races of many tongues and of fiercely conflicting religions, than a perfectly impartial, strong, just, humane government, such as that conceived, and in part administered in practice, by the best men that we have sent to India. There can be no greater glory to a country than to have produced such men, and the life-record of some of our Indian statesmen will, in every respect, bear comparison with that of any rulers that the world has shown. Unfortunately, however, financial considerations interfere, and the government, of which these admirable statesmen are the head, is, as we have seen above, brought to the door of the cottage of the cultivator by the native policeman.

Even as regards the best side of our rule, its impartiality is not, perhaps, so popular as the partiality of the native ruler. A great Indian civilian himself has said, "Every partiality of a chief, whether it be founded on class feeling, or political instinct, or religion, is likely to endear him," at all events, to some classes of his subjects. Whatever may be the case in the Presidency towns, when we "hold in India that men and women, Brahmins and Sweepers, . . . are equal before the law, are equal indeed for any purposes whatsoever, we approach a line on which our acts may easily become, in the eyes of the native community, either positively shocking or positively absurd. The theory of equality cuts right across the grain of a society where the most familiar fact, the one thing that more than any other affects all daily life and social intercourse, is the separation of all men into castes and tribes." "Against the danger of enacting rules of law unsuited to Indian societies because they are suited to societies more advanced, the existence of native states is a valuable safeguard." "Many states have adopted some of our laws, or the general spirit of them. For purposes of Indian legislation, it would be an exceedingly useful thing to inquire, which of our laws the principal native states have of their own motion adopted, and with what modifications the laws adopted are enforced." "Where native states have voluntarily adopted methods founded on our traditions, we may feel our position greatly strengthened by the convergence of view. If no unnecessary pressure be exercised, native states spontaneously tend to become admirable fields for administrative experiment, to which, in our passion for uniformity, we have in British territory too little recourse."

From the point of view of the picturesque alone, the existence of the native states is, in this colourless modern world, not to be neglected. Elsewhere all is becoming dull and uniform. In India we have still surviving, in a thriving and modern life, thoroughly consistent with our rule, and often with real loyalty to the Empress-Queen, communities which in their political institutions recall Italy of the Middle Ages, which in their religious institutions take us back to the early ages of the historical world, and which, in variety of costume and pomp of display, exceed anything which has been witnessed in other parts of the world by those who have lived in more romantic days.

INDIA

To the traveller India may be commended as, in spite of the dreariness of large parts of its landscape, on the whole, the home of the finest sights and of the most perfect natural pictures that the world can show. A May-day review in St. Petersburg does not exceed in military lustre a cavalry camp of India; while the scenery both of Southern and Central India, and, in the cold weather, of those portions of the north which are within sight of the Himalayan Range, is not to be met with within the vast dominions of the Emperor of all the Russias. The architecture of the Taj—first of all the buildings of the world in beauty—of the pearl mosque of Agra, and of the pearl mosque of Delhi, of the walls of Agra, and some of the palaces of Central India, stands before any of the architecture of the world in charm. Now that China is being, as it is called, "opened to the world," and now that Japan has destroyed, not her scenery, but everything else that was picturesque, in her rage for modernity, India

THE BRITISH EMPIRE becomes more and more the one country of the world in which the traveller can find those varied delights, natural and artificial too, which formerly he was able to look for in the Middle Kingdom and in the Land of the Rising Sun.

CHAPTER III

THE DOMINION

THAT the upper part of the continent of North America should contain side by side two territories of equal size, of which one has fifteen times the population of the other, and more than fifteen times the wealth, would at first sight seem to imply the ultimate absorption of the less rich and populous by the other, and the merger of the Canadian dominion into the neighbouring federation of the United States. On the other hand, Canada is a hard morsel to digest. She has two dominant peoples who now live in friendly fashion side by side within her constitution: the intensely Roman Catholic and French population of Lower Canada, and the United Empire Loyalists, the descendants of the men who left the colonies which now form the United States, rather than renounce their allegiance to the British Crown. Neither of these two peoples can look forward with pleasure to absorption in the United States, and sensible citizens of the great American republic are equally unwilling to look forward, on their side, to the swallowing of the country upon their north.

The United States are hardly likely to continue to grow, as compared with Canada, at the same rate in the future as they have grown in the light of this comparison in the past. Take our own emigrants, for example. Although they have left our own shores for Canadian ports in large numbers, the bulk of these emigrants undoubtedly have crossed the border, and have gone to swell the still larger emigration which took place directly to the United States. The attraction of the better labour market, and of the greater towns, the earlier development of the railways of the United States, the greater freedom of life—many attractions—concurred to

THE DOMINION

draw people to the south. But the better land of the United States has been taken up. The good land of Canada is becoming known. The Canadian winter, as it comes to be understood, is less terrifying to immigrants than it was, and Canada, although it can never rival the United States in population or in wealth, will to some extent gain in the comparisons of the future. The mineral wealth of Canada, which is now believed by the best authorities to be very great, is partly unknown in contrast with the better-known United States; but probabilities must incline us to the view that mineral development and manufacturing development will, in a not distant future, be rapid on the Canadian side of the border. The Dominion of Canada is not what it might have been if we had known what we now know at the time of the boundary negotiations with the United States; and there is no heavier charge, among all the heavy charges that may be brought against British government in relation to the colonies, than that which arises from the ignorance and neglect which were shown, both in the negotiations of 1842 and in two other cases which now concern boundaries of the same dominion.

There probably are few of my readers who need to be reassured upon the subject of the loyalty to the British connection of the French-Canadian people. Until the wretched events which occurred not long ago in South Africa, there was every reason to believe that in that part of the world a colony, of which the bulk of the inhabitants were of a foreign race, would settle down in the happiest relations between British and Dutch, and in perfect attachment to British rule. It is still our hope and belief that this will be so. If we entertain a confident anticipation of the kind, it is largely on account of our historical and personal knowledge of what has occurred in Canada. We conquered the French-Canadians at the end of a terrific struggle for mastery in the new world between Great Britain and France—a struggle which raged over Europe, India, and America, as well as the high seas. A great number of years after the conquest of Canada we had so little understood how good relations, which had been brought about for a time, should be preserved, that our French-Canadian subjects actually rose in arms for their liberties, their tongue, and their religion at the beginning of the Queen's reign. They are now, under the admirable institutions which in our late-born wisdom we have conferred upon them, perhaps the most loyal of all the peoples under the British Crown; and they are so in spite of the fact that they have remained intensely French, proud of their race and of its history, and deeply attached to their tongue and to its literature. So far is this affection carried that both the revolutionary flag and the revolutionary anthem of France are popular in Canada, in spite of the intense Roman Catholic feeling of the population. The problem which we have solved in Canada is even more difficult than that which has been solved by the same means in Switzerland. The Swiss had to bring together fierce Roman Catholics and ferocious Protestants. They had to face religious wars, extending into recent times. They had three races—German, French, and Italian—and three tongues. But their people were all Swiss in sentiment, or at least not German, for there was no Germany except the Empire, against which they had fought. Their French were not French, for there had always been a French-speaking borderland, in Switzerland, in Savoy, in Franche Comté, in Lorraine, in the bishoprics, and in the Walloon part of the seven provinces, which had not been historically French. Their Italians were not Italians, for there was no Italy. Our difficulty was equal as regards religion, and vastly greater as regards race and tongue, because the French-Canadians were, as they are, French in nationality. The double allegiance of the French Canadians in the present day—on the one hand, to the British Crown, and to the liberties which they enjoy under it, and, on the other hand, not to a foreign Power, which they regard as foreign, but to their own race and literature—is one of the most interesting spectacles that the world affords.

The desire of the French Canadians to remain French in spirit, kept them on our side during our wars with our American colonists, who were their old enemies; and it is highly probable that the Province of Quebec and the French element in the Canadian north-west will always remain rather British than American in sympathy. Their distinct institutions and their religion —virtually established in Lower Canada, and supreme in education—would be menaced by absorption in the United States with its common-school system. But there is something more than this. The French Canadians belong, not to modern or republican France, but to France of the old days of the kings and Church, before the Revolution. They are, even when they call themselves Liberals, as do the majority, and are nicknamed " Les Rouges," Conservative in turn of mind, and this is even a stronger tie to the British Crown than that which has been named above. Their conservatism of spirit forms a bond which would endure even if the common-school system should, under Roman Catholic influence, come to be modified in portions of the United States, of which, however, as yet there seems little probability. Just as the population of Alsace, of purely German race, supplies Paris with its most patriotic "French" or anti-German element, so the French population of Canada supplies the Dominion with an element as patriotically British as even the United Empire Loyalists themselves.

Upper Canada was itself settled by men who gave up their homes and a large part of their property to maintain their allegiance to the British flag; who went out into the wilderness, in the shape of unbroken forest, of what was then Western Canada, in order to remain in their own Empire. The sturdiness and energy of the United Empire original population has been thoroughly maintained, and the rivalry between the Scotch immigrants, the United Empire Loyalists, and the French Canadians, is friendly rivalry of three very distinct groups of men, all equally patriotic and well affected to our rule.

I should be going somewhat beyond the sphere of these articles, if I were to attempt to draw any analogy between a possible state of things in Ireland and the actual state of things in Lower Canada, but I may be allowed to say that we have shown, under compulsion, a successful liberality with regard to religious toleration, or something more than toleration, in the Province of Quebec, which we have never been willing to display, and are not yet prepared to grant, in the case of Roman Catholic Ireland. It is impossible to deny that the Roman Catholic Church in French Canada is not only predominant, but is actually privileged, and possesses, in fact, a stronger position than in any Roman Catholic country

THE BRITISH EMPIRE

in the world—even than in Belgium itself with its clerical administration. The Roman Catholic Church is not nominally established in Quebec, but is more powerful than is any State Church, while remaining wholly unfettered by ties imposed in Roman Catholic states—by the concordat of France, or similar laws.

It is an interesting fact that the Roman Catholic population has grown gigantically in Canada, as the French there are a prolific race. Since Federation, there has been a great decrease of that friction in the fringes of French Canada, between the Protestant and Roman Catholic population, which formerly existed; and since a very long period of Conservative rule has given place to the rule of the Canadian Liberal party under a French-speaking Prime Minister (who is, however, as eloquent in the English as in the French tongue), friction seems still further to have diminished.

The weak point in the position is that the Dominion takes insufficient military steps for its own protection. There is universal liability to military service in a militia, as in the United States; but, even more than in the United States, this is a mere paper liability, and the organized militia are, considering the immense length of the Canadian frontier, a small, as they are somewhat of a dwindling, force. It has long been the policy of successive British Governments to withdraw all troops from the Dominion except from two extreme points — Halifax and Esquimalt, which are coaling stations or naval bases for the fleet. But the great risk of Canada, in the event of war, would be in the centre of her enormous line of common frontier with the United States. The feeling in Canada upon the subject of defence is somewhat foggy. There is a strong desire for independence of policy, and for self-respecting national existence. On the other hand, there is a suspicion that anything like a policy of armament would produce distrust, and possible hostility, on the southern frontier. The cure would seem to be in a prudent and peaceful organization of the militia force, upon a scheme more similar to that which is a complete success in Switzerland, and on so purely a defensive footing, that there could be in it no possible suggestion of offence.

The strength of the Dominion may be indefinitely augmented by further mineral discoveries. The deposits of gold, of iron, and of other minerals, already known to exist within her soil, are very rich; but the most valuable of her gold-fields lies so far north, that the rigour of the climate prevents that rush of population which would elsewhere long ago have taken place. The extraordinary rapidity of the development of the far-western states of the United States, through the discovery of surface gold in California in 1848, and the subsequent continuance of quartz gold-mining in the same district, the development of Victoria, and that of the Transvaal, through similar discoveries, have shown the world what gold does for rapid increase of population, with resultant increase of agricultural prosperity, in a new country. British Columbia is full of gold, silver, copper, and coal, and the Lake Superior district of the Dominion, of silver and iron; while the discovery of gold veins in the province of Ontario is now continuous.

The Jubilee ceremonies of 1897 in London popularized the figure of Sir Wilfrid Laurier, and his speeches in Paris formed the weightiest of modern discouragement to our foes in all parts of the world. The disappointment produced in England by the speeches of the Prime Minister of New South Wales, and by the attitude of the Australian colonies with regard to the maintenance of the British fleet, were balanced by the exultation with which the people of the United Kingdom learnt the story of the Canadian Dominion.

CHAPTER IV

NEWFOUNDLAND AND FRANCE

WE have made, in recent years, considerable sacrifices for the sake of good relations with the French. We have given up our perpetual most-favoured-nation clause and low-duties treaty in Tunis to them; we have gone out of our way to expressly recognize their action in Madagascar which has led to annexation, with similar effect upon our trade; and, while in Siam we have helped them to obtain from the Siamese the recognition of their extension over a large tract of territory which was recently Siamese, in Africa we have over and over again yielded before French enterprise. There has, all the time, been pending between ourselves and

NEWFOUNDLAND AND FRANCE

France a really dangerous question, which grows more and more difficult as well as dangerous every day. If a policy of "graceful concession" is to be pursued, it is in French concession in Newfoundland that we ought to find our *quid pro quo*.

By the Treaty of Utrecht, 1713, Newfoundland became a wholly British colony, and the subjects of France were forbidden to "erect any buildings there besides stages made of boards, and huts necessary and usual for drying of fish, or to resort to the said island beyond the time necessary for fishing and drying of fish. But it shall be allowed to the subjects of France to catch fish, and to dry them on land in that part only," etc.—namely, on what was often called "the French Shore." By the Treaty of Paris of 1763, this provision as to "fishing and drying" was confirmed, and the islands of St. Pierre and Miquelon were ceded to France as a shelter for the French fishermen —the French engaging to erect no buildings upon them, except for the convenience of the fishery—a condition which they have violated. By the Treaty of Versailles of 1783, the French, to "prevent quarrels which have hitherto arisen, ... consent to renounce the right of fishing in," etc., *i.e.* varying the so-called French Shore. The King of England by a declaration promised to prevent his subjects from interrupting, by their competition, the fishery of the French during the temporary exercise of it, and promised for this purpose to cause the fixed settlements which might be found there to be removed. He also promised that the French should not be incommoded in cutting wood necessary for the repair of scaffolds, huts, and boats. On the other hand, the method of carrying on the fishery hitherto in existence, was to be the plan upon which the fishery should continue to be carried on; the French were to be forbidden to winter in Newfoundland, and were to build only scaffolds, but the British were not to molest the French during their fishing, nor to injure their scaffolds in their absence.

NEWFOUNDLAND AND FRANCE

The islands ceded were to serve as a "real shelter to the French fishermen." Mr. A. W. Harvey, one of the Newfoundland delegates who appeared at the Bar of the House of Commons, has pointed out in a Memorandum published by our Government, with the approval of the Colonial Office, that our trouble lies in the words of our own King's declaration; but if that has to be read strictly against us, we ought to read the French King's declaration strictly, and we have never held the French to its observance.

By the Treaty of Paris of 1814, the previous enactments were unhappily continued. To judge by the whole of the language employed in the negotiations and declarations, no kind of fishery was contemplated except cod-fishing, and cod were intended by the word "fish." The word "fish" in Newfoundland in the present day means cod.

In 1857 the Secretary of State for the Colonies promised that the two principles which would continue to guide the Home Government were, "that the rights at present enjoyed by the community of Newfoundland, are not to be ceded or exchanged without their assent; and that the constitutional mode of submitting measures for that assent, is by laying them before the colonial legislature." Proposed arrangements with France having been "refused by the colony will, of course, fall to the ground. You are authorized to give such assurance as you may think proper, that the consent of the community of Newfoundland is regarded by H.M.G. as the essential preliminary to any modification of their territorial or maritime rights."

Newfoundland is now a self-governing colony possessing responsible institutions, and it is, so far as I know, the only such colony over which, or any portion of which, any foreign Power claims what lawyers call a "servitude." The British Crown is admittedly sovereign in all parts of Newfoundland, including the so-called "French

NEWFOUNDLAND AND FRANCE

Shore." The colonial legislature deals by statute and by its administration with all portions of the colony, but a foreign Power has rights within the territorial waters, and, during a large portion of the year, on the actual shore of the colony, which, so far as they go, are in derogation of the usual rights of the Sovereign and of the legislature.

Under the King's declaration, British naval officers have exercised singularly arbitrary powers on the coast of Newfoundland—powers which, it may be confidently said, have often exceeded their statutory authority, and which, if the poor people concerned could have brought them before the Courts, British or Colonial, would have been severely condemned. As regards principle, however, there was no conflict between the Colonial and the British Governments until the time of the administration of 1886–92.

In 1882–83 and '84 certain British subjects had erected lobster factories at spots on the so-called French Shore, where there were no houses or buildings of any kind, and where no fisherman, either French or English, had been in the habit of fishing. In 1886 French fishermen visited the district for the purpose of catching lobsters. In 1887 a French warship cut the gear of all the British lobster-traps and set them adrift, so that they were destroyed. A British officer on the coast supported the French naval division in their action. In 1888 the captain of H.M.S. *Emerald* compelled the British lobster-catchers to move. The ground given, up to this time, was that the lobster-trawls and traps interfered with the French fishing, *i.e.* presumably the French cod-fishing.

Lord Iddesleigh in 1886 had protested in advance against the erection of French lobster factories, in these words, addressed to M. Waddington: "I have to express the hope that the French naval officers will make known to the persons concerned, that such a course is not allowed by the treaties,

NEWFOUNDLAND AND FRANCE

and must be discontinued." It is a pity that these words were not stood to by our Government. In July, 1888, Lord Knutsford informed Lord Salisbury that the construction of lobster factories then commenced by the French, and the asserted claim to grant to French subjects lobster concessions, "are clearly contrary to treaty."

It was in 1888 that some French subjects set up a claim that two British subjects, Murphy and Andrews, were violating the treaties by taking and canning lobsters on the so-called French Shore, and that French subjects, and French only, had the right to take and can lobsters on that shore, and to erect upon British territory factories or establishments for the purpose of preserving lobsters. This subject at once grew into a prominence which has dwarfed all other developments of the Newfoundland question.

In September, 1888, we addressed to France a note calling attention to the illegality of French lobster-packing factories.

THE BRITISH EMPIRE

The French Government several times stated that these factories were temporary, and, with regard to some of them, they said they had been suppressed. As a matter of fact, they continued to exist, and a fresh protest was made by Lord Salisbury, at the end of 1888 and beginning of 1889, against "an assumption of territorial rights in derogation of the sovereignty of the British Crown." The French Government then, for the first time, set up an entirely new contention—that lobsters were fish, and, apparently, that their factories were legal. Arbitration was first proposed by Lord Salisbury in 1889, when the Newfoundland Government absolutely refused the arbitration suggested. In May, 1890, the Foreign Office informed the Government of France, that they could not admit the contention that French naval officers can have a right to interfere with British fishermen, in the territorial waters of a British colony; but, nevertheless, the French have continued to do so up to the present time.

NEWFOUNDLAND AND FRANCE

The Newfoundland shore cod-fisheries, which alone were contemplated by the treaties, are so unimportant as compared with those of the Great Bank south of Newfoundland, open to all nations, that only seven French boats fish on the so-called French Shore, as against the hundreds which fit out, either in Flanders, Picardy, Normandy, Brittany, or St. Pierre and Miquelon, to prosecute the fishery on the Bank. The lobster-canning industry, on the other hand, is a lucrative one; and unfortunately, although in theory we have always asserted that lobsters are not fish under the treaty, that the scaffolding for drying cod contemplated by the treaties cannot cover lobster-canning factories, and that moreover, in any case, we have a concurrent right of fishery with that of France on the so-called French Shore, yet British naval officers interfered, along with the French, to cause the removal of establishments erected by British subjects for the purpose of taking and canning lobster. This action on the part of the British officers has been distinctly held to be illegal by the Courts, both in first instance and on appeal. It is really monstrous, after the direct prohibition by the Treaty of Utrecht of the erection of buildings by the French, except those "necessary and usual for the drying of fish" (while all the later documents speak of the fishery assigned by the Treaty of Utrecht, and declare that the future method of carrying it on shall be the primeval method of carrying it on), to then pretend that lobster-canning is included in the words used to cover the drying of cod. Instead of protecting British fishermen, in the prosecution of their lawful avocation, and resisting the new claim of the French, our Government, after failing to enforce the claim of the French, tried to go to arbitration upon it before a Court in which the best known personage was to have been M. de Martens, the hereditary librarian of the Russian Foreign Office, whose opinion on such points was hardly likely to be impartial.

NEWFOUNDLAND AND FRANCE

Luckily the French added a condition, the enormity of which was such that the arbitration has never taken place, and it may be hoped now never will.

While British officers were backed up by the Government, in most arbitrary action, on behalf of the French and against the colonists, the theory continued to be that the French pretensions were disputed by us. At the end of 1889 the home Government sent for the Prime Minister of Newfoundland, who came to England in 1890. A *modus vivendi* was agreed to, preserving such British lobster factories as existed, and the French Government agreeing that they would undertake to grant no new lobster-fishing concessions "on fishing grounds occupied by British subjects," whatever that might mean. But the limitation was afterwards explained away, and the *modus vivendi* stated to mean the *status quo*. The colonial Government strongly protested against the *modus vivendi*, as a virtual admission of a concurrent right of lobster fishing prejudicial to the position of Newfoundland in future negotiation; and there can be no doubt that the adoption of the *modus vivendi* by the British Government without previous reference to the colony, and against its wish, was a violation of the principle laid down by the then Mr. Labouchere, when Secretary of State in 1857, and by Lord Palmerston. Our Government deny this, because they expressly reserved all questions of principle and right in the agreement with the French, and that is so, of course; but there can be no doubt about the effect of what they did.

By an answer given by an Under-Secretary of State in the House of Commons, the views of the Newfoundland Government were misrepresented, it being stated that they "were consulted as to the terms of the *modus vivendi*, which was modified to some extent to meet their views, although concluded without reference to them in its final shape;" but the Newfoundland Government insisted that the terms of the *modus vivendi* had not

NEWFOUNDLAND AND FRANCE

been modified in accordance with their views, as they had protested against the whole arrangement. The home Government quibbled and said that the answer showed that the Newfoundland Government were not responsible for the *modus vivendi* as settled. Plain people, however, must continue to be as indignant as the colonists are at the misrepresentation and the breach of Mr. Labouchere's principle.

The terms of the *modus vivendi* accord to unfounded pretensions the standing of reasonable claims, and confer upon the French the actual possession and enjoyment of the rights to which these claims relate. Mr. Baird refused to comply with the *modus vivendi*. Sir Baldwin Walker, commanding on the coast, landed a party of bluejackets in 1891 and took the law into his own hands against Mr. Baird, was sued for damages and twice lost his case. There had been an Imperial Act under which Sir Baldwin Walker might have been protected, but it had been repealed when self-government was granted to Newfoundland. In the same year of 1891 a Newfoundland Act was passed, under heavy pressure from the Home Government, compelling colonial subjects to observe the instructions of the naval officers to the extent of at once quitting the French shore if directed, and the Act was to be in force till the end of 1893. The home Government had passed a Bill through the House of Lords, brought it to the House of Commons, and dropped it, before it received the royal assent, only after the Prime Minister of Newfoundland had been heard at the Bar of both Houses and had promised colonial legislation. The French Government have insisted that a British Act should be passed; and Lord Salisbury, while declaring that there ought to be a permanent Colonial Act, has always refused to promise a British Act. To my mind, the Newfoundland people went too far in giving up their freedom by passing the Act which I have named, an Act to which, had I been a member of the Newfoundland legislature, nothing would have induced me to consent; and my sympathies are entirely with the Newfoundlanders in their refusal to part with their freedom, for all time, by making so monstrous a statute permanent.

The French maintain, to use the words of the French Minister of Marine of 1888, writing to the Minister of Foreign Affairs, that the rights of France on the so-called French Shore, are "nothing else than a part of her ancient sovereignty over the island which she retained while ceding the soil to England—rights which she has never alienated." The island is about the oldest of British colonies, with about the oldest of British colonial representative institutions. France never possessed the sovereignty of which her Minister of Marine has spoken. But the Newfoundland Act reads like a consecration of this pretended sovereignty, and it makes British naval officers the policemen, and more than the policemen—the autocratic or Russian policemen—of the French.

THE BRITISH EMPIRE

There has been nothing to choose between the action of the two parties in the Newfoundland question, and the policy of the Colonial Office has been marked by an unpleasant continuity. When Lord Ripon became Secretary of State in 1892, he began to press the Colonial Ministry for permanent legislation, just as it is said that the Colonial Office is pressing them at the present time. In pressing for permanent coercive legislation the Colonial Office threatens Imperial legislation, which would receive in the House of Lords the consent of both parties, but which it is certain that, in the interest of our colonial empire, Government ought not to be allowed to carry through the House of Commons.

The Newfoundland Government has pointed out that the permanent legislation asked for, is desired in part for the enforcement of an ultimate award of a proposed arbitration relative to the lobster question, agreed on between the Foreign Office and the Government of France, but from the outset opposed by the colony, the agreement having been made, not only without its consent, but in despite of its frequently expressed opposition. Ultimately, however, "in view of the probable opposition to an Imperial Bill in the House of Commons," Lord Ripon proposed to invite the colonial legislature to renew the temporary Act for two years. The Newfoundland Government then agreed to re-enact the temporary Bill for one year without prejudice to their position. This proposal was refused by Lord Ripon, and the colonial Government then gave way. The temporary Act has since been again and again renewed.

It is pretended that the British squadron on the coast of Newfoundland protects British subjects, in the exercise of their rights, against unlawful acts on the part of the French. But judging by the actions of British officers, their instructions, which are secret, must be in absolute antagonism to the declarations of our statesmen in their despatches. Where a Frenchman commits an act of violence against a British subject, by destroying his boat or fishing-gear, the British subject can find in practice no remedy, as the case is reported by the officer in command of the British ship on the station to the Admiral, by the Admiral to the Admiralty, by the Admiralty to the Foreign Office, and by the Foreign Office to the Ambassador in Paris with instructions to submit the matter to the French Government. The French Government then refuses redress, and the matter comes back again through the same channel. Where the case arises upon land the British subject complains to the Governor, the Governor to the Colonial Office, the Colonial Office to the Foreign Office, and the Foreign Office to the Admiralty, for it to be referred to the Naval Officer on the station for report; the Officer on the station returns it through the Admiral to the Admiralty, the Admiralty to the Foreign Office, the Foreign Office to the

NEWFOUNDLAND AND FRANCE

British Ambassador in Paris, and then back as before, in the invariable form: "H.M.G. regret that they are unable to obtain from the French authorities a recognition of the claim." The pretensions of the French officers on the so-called French Shore are unbounded, extending to the point of ordering British vessels out of British waters, where they are merely using the harbour and coast — the absolute possession of which by Great Britain is acknowledged by the Treaty of Utrecht. Seven hundred miles of coast of a British colony become a no-man's-land, with no security of any sort against arbitrary rule by foreign naval officers, and mines are undeveloped, on account of the dog-in-the-manger policy pursued, not because the fishery is of the slightest value in itself, or really exercised, but because we happen to have other difficulties with France—in Africa, for example—for which the Newfoundland colonists are certainly not responsible. The French Government have granted concessions to

French subjects to engage in industry upon portions of British soil, nominally governed by British magistrates, and represented by members in the Colonial legislature. The French insist that their right of fishing on the so-called French shore is absolute and not concurrent; yet we granted similar rights, at one time, to the United States in similar words, and this right was always held in practice to be concurrent and not exclusive. The French have gone so far, in the words of M. Flourens when Foreign Minister, as to assert that the so-called French Shore "ought to have remained uninhabited." We may agree with the French so far as this: that under any other circumstances than the coast of this British colony being desert, the Newfoundland contention is a true one—that the French rights are "anomalous and intolerable."

The temporary Act which we have bullied the colony into passing is a shameful Act, without precedent or parallel in the British Empire. In the words of one of the leading statesmen of Newfoundland, it is one "by which the liberties and property of our people were made subject to the will of naval officers . . . acting under instructions from the British Government." Under it, British subjects can be arrested and deported from the soil of a self-governing colony, to another part of the colony, before trial and without appeal. The whole story is one of abdication of rights in consequence of threats. No such state of things would be tolerated in the case of any other self-governing colony; and we have only to ask ourselves what we should do, if the Newfoundlanders had the spirit of the Australians, in order to convince ourselves of this fact.

Newfoundland, which is poor and backward as compared with the other self-governing colonies, has frequently been solicited to come into Canadian federation, for it is the only portion of British North America not included within the Dominion. It has hitherto declined, but will probably end by agreeing, and anything which can widen its interests, and which may thus improve its politics, will be a boon to Newfoundland.

CHAPTER V

THE COMMONWEALTH OF AUSTRALIA

THERE is nothing more striking in the history of the British Colonies in North America than the fact that when what are now the United States were mainly British, and what is now Canada was mainly French, every far-sighted observer recognized, from one hundred and fifty years ago up to the American Revolution, that it was the presence of the French in Canada which was the essential condition of the maintenance of British rule on the American continent. A well-known passage in the work of a Swedish traveller, written in 1748, prophesies the constitution by "the English colonies in America," of "a separate state entirely independent of England." This traveller saw that the colonies being threatened by the French, and the British commanding the sea, there was "reason to regard the French in North America as the chief power which urges" the "colonies to submission." Later in the century Montcalm, as quoted by Mr. Hugh Egerton, consoled himself for his defeat by the reflection that the loss of Canada would be "of more service to my country than a victory."

The strongest reason which urges even the most advanced of native-born Australians to accept British rule is somewhat similar to that which long kept the American colonies steadfast to their allegiance. It is recognized that the command of the sea by the British Power is necessary to the peace and freedom of Australia; and the Metropolis, having hitherto received from the Australian colonies but a scanty contribution towards the cost of the fleet, has frequently urged upon the colonies the adoption of common measures of defence, the need for which has become a main factor in promoting the growth of federal feeling. No one can doubt that if the Australian colonies should remain permanently separated from one another by customs-frontiers, with tariffs directed against one another's goods, and with other grounds of quarrel afforded by such questions as the use of the waters of the Murray for irrigation purposes, fratricidal wars between them are not impossible in the future. There might be renewed in Australia the history of the relations of England with Scotland, with Ireland, and with Wales; or that, in this century, of the former Spanish colonies in South America, which, in spite of their common tongue, common religion, and common tradition of risings for the sake of liberty against the mother-country, have not avoided terrible internecine wars.

The wise legislation of the Imperial Parliament long ago established for Australia, with the addition of New Zealand, and of the Crown Colony of Fiji, the Federal

Council of Australasia. But the steady refusal of the mother-colony—New South Wales—to come into this assembly, deprived it of all authority, and in the long run almost of very life itself.

The chief men of the colonies, in spite of a powerful self-interest leading most of them to dread absorption in the new and unknown life of a larger State, had long recognized in theory the necessity of Confederation, and in 1897 an admirable Bill was fought out in every detail by a Conference convened for the purpose, in which all the Australian colonies at one moment were represented, all but one represented for most of the time, and all but two (lying at the two extremities) represented throughout the entire period. The Commonwealth Bill was completed in the first month of the present year; and submitted to a popular vote in the most important colonies on the 3rd and 4th of June.

In the vote, while Victoria, South Australia and Tasmania adopted the Commonwealth

Constitution by overwhelming majorities, New South Wales voted in its favour by a small majority, but the measure did not receive in the mother-colony the number of votes which, owing to the influence of the opponents of the Bill in its Parliament, had been made a necessary condition of its passing. The resistance of the Labour party and the lukewarm support of the Prime Minister, Mr. Reid, were probably owing to the unpopularity of the conditions which had been found necessary to prevent opposition on the part of the smaller colonies. The permission granted to the smaller colonies, by the constitution of the Commonwealth, to be represented in its Senate by the same number of members as are accorded to the great colonies, Victoria and New South Wales, has led to much suspicion as to the probable working of the Bill on the part of the democratic element in all the colonies. On the other hand, when the proposed Senate is rigidly scrutinized, it is difficult to see on what grounds the democracy base their fear of that body. It would at least be possible that if such a Senate were brought into existence it might be found to be a more advanced body than the Chamber of Representatives. It is possible, however, that, although there are few Conservative safeguards to be found in the law creating it, the mere name of Senate will of itself confer moderation upon those who are brought within so august a body.

In a speech before the vote was taken, Mr. Reid, Prime Minister of New South Wales, stated that if the Bill were defeated he should not despair of federation, but would propose that New South Wales should join the present Federal Council. It becomes, therefore, of some interest to examine what that Federal Council is. Created by an Act of 1885, and brought into existence on the recommendation of four colonies (in the Act styled provinces) shortly afterwards, the Federal Council of Australasia consists of two representatives

COMMONWEALTH OF AUSTRALIA

from each of the self-governing colonies who choose to be represented on it, and of one from Fiji, and from any other Crown Colony which may at any future time come into existence within the boundaries named, *i.e.* in New Guinea. The main power conferred on the Council was that of legislating in regard to the relations of Australasia with the islands of the Pacific, but it has power to deal with all matters referred to it by the various legislatures, subject to the subsequent adoption of the Acts by the legislatures themselves. The hostility of New South Wales it was which paralyzed the Federal Council. If New South Wales should now come into it, and the other colonies should be willing to waive for the moment the adoption of the Commonwealth Bill, which can be brought into existence by the action of three of them, or if, while three of the colonies desire the Constitution of the Commonwealth, the Secretary of State and Parliament decide that it is better to wait for the action of New South Wales, then the Federal Council, with the warm co-operation of the colonial parliaments, may serve the main end of the practical Constitution of a Federal Government.

The Federal Council, however, having no Executive, though Prime Ministers of the Colonies have sat upon it, and might all sit upon it, having no judiciary, no control of funds, no Ministry, will always be inferior in authority to the Commonwealth which some of the colonies so warmly favour, and which, on the whole, is favoured by a large majority of the entire Australian people.

Sooner or later, there can be little doubt, the Commonwealth Act will be brought into operation. The governors of the various colonies, at present appointed by the Crown, will then be virtually superseded by a single Crown officer—the Governor-General. The Senate which, as stated above, will be composed of an equal number of members for each colony, in the Bill called States, will be elected for six years, half retiring every three years, but will be elected by the whole colony as a single electorate. The latter of these two provisions is intensely democratic; and in my opinion more than a set-off to the Labour party and the democracy against the slightly anti-democratic tendency of the former of the provisions.

Much fighting took place in the Convention over the clauses dealing with the origin and progress of money Bills. The Senate has been given power in regard to money Bills more considerable than those of the House of Lords; and the position of the Imperial House of Commons as sole keeper of the public purse has been contrasted with the proposals of the Commonwealth Bill, for the purpose of damaging the latter. While ordinary money Bills must originate in the House of Representatives, it is provided that a proposed law shall not be treated as a money Bill by reason of its containing proposals for fees, and, what is more important, a power is given to the

Senate to return to the House of Representatives any money Bill, requesting by message the omission or amendment of any items or provisions therein. It is also provided that tax laws shall deal with one subject of taxation only, so that an opportunity is given to the Senate of throwing out a money Bill essential to the taxation of the year, without appearing to reject the whole finance measure in such a way as to bring the national existence to a stop. The power of the Senate to send messages to the House suggesting alterations in Bills which it cannot amend is taken from the constitution of South Australia.

To bring the question between the Australian Labour party and the Convention to a sharp issue, it may be pointed out that Sir William Harcourt's Finance Bill would not have passed the House of Lords with his Death Duties proposals in it if the House of Lords had held the position given to the Senate in the Commonwealth Constitution.

COMMONWEALTH OF AUSTRALIA

It was supposed that the Commonwealth proposals were likely to break down upon finance or upon the much-vexed question of the seat of government, but it may safely be asserted that the hesitation of New South Wales (which proved to be the main obstacle in the way) was caused almost entirely by the difficulty which we have been discussing of the undue powers given, in the opinion of the New South Wales democracy, to the smaller states, and especially by the provisions with regard to the Senate put in for their benefit. I cannot, however, but think that these matters have been discussed in New South Wales as though the Senate were a House of squatters—a House of rich men, a House of Lords, and I think that the provisions of the Bill make it probable that the Senate will be a somewhat democratic assembly.

A curious struggle arose in the third session of the Convention, at Melbourne, in the present year over the name of the federal capital. The Bill is "the Commonwealth of

Australia Bill." Clause 124 provides that the seat of government of the Commonwealth—that is, of the Commonwealth of Australia—shall be determined by the Commonwealth Parliament; and the colonies which had some intention of remaining outside the Commonwealth, such as Queensland and Western Australia, complained that the Commonwealth intended, in Sir John Forrest's words, "to collar the name" of Australia. If there were any prospect of a Commonwealth being formed without New South Wales, or still more without New South Wales, Queensland, and Western Australia, it would be no doubt ridiculous for three colonies (two of them small in geographical extent, although one of these two is populous, rich, and well provided with considerable statesmen) to assume for their capital the name of the capital of the Commonwealth of Australia. It is, however, obvious that the Commonwealth cannot come into existence until at least New South Wales, failing Queensland and Western

COMMONWEALTH OF AUSTRALIA

Australia, is within it, and that fresh negotiations must continue for the purpose of bringing her in, as a majority of the electors voting, even in New South Wales, desire.

Little importance seems to have been attached, in the discussions before the constituencies, to those proposals with regard to future alteration of the constitution, which gave rise in the Convention to debates of the highest interest. The clause inserted to provide for the case of South Australia, which has adult suffrage, and of any other states which may adopt it, is one through which a coach and four could easily be driven. It declares that, until the qualification of electors becomes uniform throughout the Commonwealth, only one half the electors voting for and against a proposed law for the amendment of the Constitution shall be counted in the case of adult-suffrage states. It is obvious at a glance that this is a rough-and-ready proposal, and that a state adopting fancy franchises, for women, for example, would not have its weight accurately determined under the clause, as compared with a state having manhood suffrage only. It will, however, be possible under the Constitution for the Commonwealth to create a uniform suffrage, but it will only be able to do this if it gives to every state the suffrage of South Australia, *i.e.* the widest.

An interesting provision of the Constitution is, that power is given under certain circumstances to dissolve the Senate; and the Commonwealth Constitution is the only English Constitution, with the exception of that of South Australia, in which the Senate can be dissolved.

Mr. Reid is evidently unwilling to forfeit his present position of power in New South Wales until he sees an equal federal position within his grasp. The Conservative strain in Mr. Barton prevented him, at the recent election, from sweeping the colony for a federal Protectionist party; and Mr. Reid still unites the Radicals, the Free Traders, the Labour men, and those who, for business reasons, connected with the predominance of Sidney, and other local grounds, are real anti-federalists. Sydney, of course, fears the loss of its position, and its merchants dislike the prospect of the federal tariff. The New South Wales Labour members revolt against a constitution which does not, upon the surface, and obviously, give them what they want. Victoria is still dreaded as a rival, and so much disliked that the completeness of the federal triumph in Victoria angers even the friends of federalism across the border.

Western Australia had no real intention of joining the Commonwealth at once, and attended the Convention for the purpose of resisting Radical influences, and so moulding the constitution that it should be more to her taste, when the day comes that she may wish to unite with the other colonies.

All politicians in Australia are now either favourable to Federation, or sufficiently frightened, if opposed to it, by the powerful current in its favour, to declare that it is only to the particular provisions of the Commonwealth Bill that they are opposed, while they are favourable to the principle. It is, however, improbable that any number of fresh Conventions will be able to make, with good effect, any large changes in the Commonwealth Bill. It has been thought out with the greatest care, and what are called, in the large colonies, its defects are the necessary concessions to bring the small ones within the Commonwealth. The only other plan for bringing them in would be that pursued in Canada, namely, lavish gifts of money or the equivalents of money.

The position of the Free Traders is, of course, a difficult one, as they have at present one great colony which, after trying Protection, has returned to Free Trade, while under Federation the Commonwealth as a whole will pursue a Protectionist policy. On the other hand, they may fairly argue, and many of them do, that intercolonial

COMMONWEALTH OF AUSTRALIA

Free Trade will in the long run give them the practical blessings of Free Trade, and, as regards many branches of commerce, will tend towards actual Free Trade itself.

CHAPTER VI

NEW ZEALAND

NEW ZEALAND is a colony of extraordinary interest from a great number of different points of view. It has wondrous natural beauty, fiords finer than those of Norway, snowy alps rising from the sea and sending glaciers down to the region of the giant ferns, volcanoes, and lovely lakes. The great length of the islands from north to south produces a wonderful variety of climate; the north part, lost in the seas, being but 34° from the equator, while the extreme south is within the range of the winds which sweep the cold seas of the Antarctic region. Then, too, there are protected islands which carry the New Zealand government into 29° south latitude. The isolated

NEW ZEALAND

position of the country prevents great extremes of heat or cold. New Zealand has one of the finest of aboriginal populations—full of eloquence, but with a practical business side well developed. It is, as regards white settlement, rapidly advancing in numbers and prosperity. New Zealand, although largely settled by the younger sons of good family from England, has produced the most democratic Labour legislation existing in the world, and it has shared with South Australia that adult suffrage of which it has made a far longer trial. New Zealand is better off than any other colony as regards books about itself, and a whole library of volumes has been written upon the colony. Its scenery has no doubt proved the attraction to authors which has brought about this result.

To those who would learn the story of New Zealand's past, there may be recommended that colonial classic "Old New Zealand" by A Pakeha Maori; and, to those who would learn about its present, the speeches, pamphlets, and a little book of the present Agent-General, the Hon. W. P. Reeves, lately Minister of Labour.

New Zealand has been longer ruled by a Radical and Labour Government than has been the case with any other colony; and the Seddon Administration, continuing the Ballance Administration, after the death of Mr. Ballance, has given a considerable uniformity to the legislative proposals of the Government for a great number of years past. There has been all along, from the earliest days of the prominence of New Zealand Radicalism, much prophecy of evil from the large settlers. Sir George Grey, after being the famous Captain Grey of Australian exploration, and the still more famous Governor of the Cape and of New Zealand, retired from the Colonial Office service, and became Prime Minister of the island colony in which he had previously represented the mother country. His teaching aroused the New Zealand democracy, whose interest soon came to be watched over by men of a ruder type. Mr. Seddon had himself represented the miners of the west coast of the South Island, and well knew their wants. He would, perhaps, hardly have been capable of expressing them in well-thought-out legislation but for the assistance which he received from men such as Mr. Reeves, the continuer of the spirit of Mr. Ballance. Although the democratic legislation pointed to has been sweeping, the prophecies of evil have not come true. There has been a marvellous increase, even in those classes of production which represent the great industries based on capital. The export of wool and of meat has increased at a gigantic pace, and gloomy predictions as to the discouragement of the investment of capital have proved fallacious. At the same time, the immense efforts which have been made to promote small farming have led to a wonderfully rapid development of agricultural cultivation.

A good deal of the legislation of New Zealand resembles legislation which has been proposed in other colonies; but New Zealand has adopted a far greater proportion of the total stock of Radical propositions than has been the case elsewhere. Its temperance legislation connects itself with that of the Dominion and of some of the Australian colonies. Its school legislation is closely connected with that of Australia and of the Dominion Province of Ontario. But in its land legislation, and especially in compulsory measures with a view to the acquisition of great estates and their sub-division, New Zealand has been imitated by Australian colonies, which have not as yet attained the success in these experiments which their initiator has met with.

It must not be supposed that there is any close resemblance of conditions between New Zealand and Australia. The distance between them is considerable, being almost that which separates the Channel from Gibraltar; but the climatic differences are far greater than might be expected from even such distances. The heated interior of

NEW ZEALAND

Australia, the absence of high mountains, the consequent want of water, are all of them conditions entirely opposite to those which exist in New Zealand; and New Zealand is certainly far more like Japan than it is like Australia. Tasmania and a portion of the Gippsland peninsula in Victoria, alone of the other South Sea colonies, in the least remind us of any parts of the islands of New Zealand.

The Labour legislation of New Zealand has been so frequently described, that it may, perhaps, be enough to say that New Zealand stands in advance of most other countries in her factory legislation—especially its provisions against sweating, and in her shops and shop-assistants legislation. New Zealand also stands in front as regards her merchant seamen and shipping legislation—particularly in the existence of a manning scale, unknown elsewhere except in Norway. In reference to the last-named subject, it may in these days, when the decline of British seamen is being noticed

THE BRITISH EMPIRE

and the British shipowners are being urged to carry apprentices, be worth pointing out that by New Zealand law sailing vessels engaged in intercolonial trade have to carry apprentices or boys; so that provision is made for young seamen learning their trade, such as is not made in the mother country, and such as does not, as a fact, exist in her enormous merchant fleet. The land legislation of New Zealand has also attracted a good deal of attention, and is fairly familiar to those at home who take interest in such matters.

The colony of New Zealand has gone much further than any other in the direction of recognition of the principle of State-ownership of the soil, with tenancy rather than freehold in the occupier under the State. The Crown lands are disposed of on long lease, the State reaping the advantage of unearned increment through a progressive land tax. By an Act of 1892 small Farm Associations were established, and these are often confused with Village Settlements

NEW ZEALAND

under Mr. Ballance's Act of 1886—which has been imitated in South Australia, and now in Queensland. A new system, known as that of the Improved Farm Settlements, is now taking the place of both the others. The size of the holdings under the new system averages about one hundred acres, and these small farms are let on lease in perpetuity at a rental which covers the cost of clearing the land from forest (which is done by the State employing labour directly) together with a fair rental for the land. In 1892 New Zealand commenced the system of purchasing large estates from private individuals, for subdivision; and in 1894 these powers were made compulsory. Advances are made to settlers at a low rate of interest, and have had the effect of bringing down the rate of interest generally on mortgages in the colony.

In spite of the interest with which the labour and the land legislation of New Zealand have been viewed, and the attention which has been excited by the functions of the State being regarded with more favour in New Zealand than even in those Australian colonies in which they had been previously the most wide, the working of adult suffrage in New Zealand is probably the matter at present connected with that colony which arouses most interest in other portions of the world.

In the mother-country and in several of our greater colonies proposals have been made at various times, since Mill moved his famous amendment on Disraeli's Reform Bill, to give to some women a limited political franchise. In 1869 I suggested the restoration to women of the municipal vote, which by the Municipal Reform Act of 1835 they had lost; and this was carried. An impetus was thus given to proposals for conferring upon women a Parliamentary vote, similar to the municipal vote which had been re-created in their favour. Ever since the beginning of the 1892 Parliament, I have brought in, year by year, a Bill which would confer the suffrage upon all grown men and women—the very Bill which has recently become law in South Australia. But there are few persons in this country who are as yet ready to frankly accept the principle of a really universal franchise.

The same was the case, apparently, in all the colonies for many years. Proposals were made there, as here, to give the franchise to certain classes of women, but a franchise narrower than that conferred on men. These proposals never in any case became law. Suddenly, in 1893, in New Zealand, every grown person resident one year in the colony, and three months in one district, was enfranchised; and the Maori women were at the same time enfranchised for the election of the Maori members of the House. It is a remarkable fact that all opposition to this great change instantaneously disappeared. Close upon ninety per cent. of all the grown women of New Zealand are electors, and in the majority of the larger towns the women voters outnumber the men. They vote in almost as large a proportion as the men, and in three out of the four largest towns in New Zealand at the last election greatly more women than men went to the poll. Of those who supported and of those who opposed the reform, both classes have been surprised. It has failed to bring about any marked alteration in the political circumstances of the country. The temperance party forced on the change, but they have not been much pleased by its results, for the women have voted pretty much as their men-folk voted before, and the Conservatives and the Liberals opposed to Prohibition have received as much proportional support from the women voters as have the Prohibitionists. On the other hand, there can be no doubt that the interest of women in politics has been aroused, that a great impulse has been given to the education of women, and to their participation in public affairs, the conduct of which they have improved. In New Zealand, as in South Australia, the enfranchisement of the women has not helped that alliance of

Churches — the Church of England, the Roman Catholic Church, and the Wesleyan Church — which has worked against the secular education system of the colony.

Just as the Dominion of Canada best illustrates the triumph of self-government, and of the liberal principles applied to our colonial system by the wisdom of modern times, and just as Ceylon best illustrates the enterprise of men of our race in a tropical colony, so New Zealand may stand with these two, on at least an equal footing, as showing what can be done by the British peoples, under favourable conditions of climate and of soil, for the development of an admirable modern community. The administration which has carried the greater portion of the recent legislation of New Zealand may be upset by the so-called Conservative forces of the country, but their work will not be undone. On the contrary, it will be continued by their successors. Many of what at first were looked upon as daring experiments are now thoroughly rooted in the land; for example, the Life Insurance department of the State, the Public Trust Office, and Compulsory Industrial Arbitration. The enterprise which the colonists showed when, after the failure of the mother-country to put down the great native rising, the Imperial troops were withdrawn, and the war handed over to the colonists, who soon brought it to a peaceful end, has been steadily continued throughout the later history of the islands. New Zealand has been fortunate in the constitution of her race. The settlers were, perhaps, a better amalgam than those of the Australian colonies. The race is thoroughly good: education now universal; the average of wealth perhaps the highest in the world: the absence of immense fortunes complete. In an outdoor climate the British New Zealanders lead an outdoor life, and their horsiness and athleticism has, perhaps, been one main cause why their marvellous scenery has not as yet developed among them either literature or art. New Zealand will

NEW ZEALAND

have to work out her future for herself. She is too remote from and too different from Australia to be brought into Australian Federation, and is consequently inclined to closer direct ties with the mother-country, although not actively excited in favour of any modification of her present political position.

CHAPTER VII

AFRICA

It is perhaps convenient to treat Africa, in its connection with the British Empire, by itself, instead of picking out the two self-governing colonies—the Cape and Natal, and then treating the rest of Africa under the heading of Crown Colonies. The Governor of the Cape is High Commissioner in South Africa, and has great powers over the Crown Colonies and Protectorates, south of the Zambesi. The Chartered Company which rules Rhodesia, south of the Zambesi, under his supervision, has dominions and influence north of the Zambesi, over protectorates—one of which, though administered by the Foreign Office, is virtually a colony; and thus we

AFRICA

are brought northward to the former dominions of the Sultan of Zanzibar, half of which are now also British, and, like Nyassaland, under the Foreign Office for the present. The four Crown Colonies of the West Coast of Africa, with the Protectorates and Spheres of Influence connected with them, are detached from our South African and East African possessions, but the problems which the possession of them involves are somewhat similar to those presented by some of our South and East Africa dependencies. Our relations with the French over our supposed Sphere of Influence on the White Nile, which connects itself with our Uganda and British East Africa Protectorates, are inextricably entwined with our relations with the French in the back country of Lagos and the Niger sphere in the direction of Lake Tchad. Our White Nile Sphere of Influence, which is a somewhat shadowy extension, to the northwest, of our British East Africa Protectorates, brings us also into a conflict of tendencies with Abyssinia which is the neighbour of our Somaliland Protectorate, of which indeed a slice has just been ceded to Abyssinia. This Protectorate is under Aden—which is Indian, as a statutory part of the Government of Bombay. Three African islands are also British dependencies—St. Helena, which is a colony; Ascension, which is rated as a ship, being under the management of the Admiralty; and Socotra (on the other side of Africa, at the entrance to the Gulf of Aden), which is a dependency of Aden.

The first observation which occurs to one to make upon our heterogeneous dominions in Africa, is that some simplicity might be brought into our administration, both at home and across the seas, if the whole of them were declared colonies or colonial protectorates, and placed under the Colonial Office. The present distinctions are impossible to justify, as they are difficult to explain. The complexity introduced into administration by Mr. Rhodes and his

AFRICA

shareholders, as regards their interests south of the Zambesi, being dealt with by the Colonial Office, and as regards their interests north of the Zambesi dealt with by the Foreign Office, is amazing. The Foreign Office has in British Central Africa the administration of what is called a Protectorate, where there is in its central portions no vestige of any native government to protect, and what is in fact an ordinary colony, as regards which there is no conceivable reason to be suggested why it should not be under the Colonial Office rather than under the Foreign Office. In Uganda the Foreign Office has had to deal with questions of administration, with risings, and with the conduct of wars, for which it is not organized, and which distract it from its diplomatic work. The Niger Company and the Oil Rivers Protectorate have hitherto been under the Foreign Office, while Lagos, which is mixed up with them in its interests, has been under the Colonial Office. It is understood that in recent military operations the sphere of the Niger Company has been virtually removed to Colonial Office control. Negotiations are on foot, though this was denied in the House of Commons as late as April, for the purchase of the territorial and administrative rights of the Niger Company; and when the purchase has been carried through, no doubt the whole of the district, including the Oil Rivers Protectorate, will be transferred to the Colonial Office, and possibly even brought under a single administration with the colony of Lagos.

Cape Colony, by far the larger of the two self-governing colonies in Africa, is, to a great extent, if not mainly, Dutch. Natal, the other, is intensely British. In Cape Colony a happy fusion of the political aspirations of the races had come about, as in Canada, before the Jameson raid, which put a sudden end for a time to these good relations. The effect, however, of the raid is wearing off, and there are already signs that the violent suspicions of the extreme

AFRICA

Dutch, on the one hand, and the somewhat blatant imperialism of the extreme British element, on the other, are again giving way to a more reasonable consideration of common interests. The South African Republic, or Transvaal as it is commonly called, is, of course, a self-governing Dutch-Afrikander state,—absolutely uncontrolled as regards its purely domestic affairs, except by a vestige of interference in some matters which concern the aboriginal natives, but unable to make treaties or to be officially represented at foreign Courts, and, in other words, subject to a general control, on our part, of its foreign relations. Its situation may be compared in this respect with that occupied towards India by the States of Afghanistan and Nepal. The Orange Free State is a Dutch Afrikander Republic, still more independent, constitutionally and theoretically speaking, of us, but not disturbed to the same extent by the presence in its midst of a fiercely British minority, as is the Transvaal, and, therefore, on the

THE BRITISH EMPIRE

whole, as regards its rulers, more friendly to us. I have called the extreme British element in the Transvaal a minority, although I am aware that many think, mistakenly, that it is a majority in that country which is kept down by force. The foreign or non-Dutch element in the Transvaal is very large and very rich, but the dominant sentiment is not pro-British, although it is anti-Dutch. The balance of the scale is turned by a strong American and Jewish element, which desires to retain a republican constitution and to avoid merger in a British colony; but which is even more opposed than is the purely British element to the old-fashioned Dutch.

Powerful among the British in South Africa, Mr. Rhodes, virtually governing Rhodesia, and influential north of the Zambesi through his telegraphs and his subsidies, looks forward to the connection of British Central Africa, by Lake Tanganyika, with Lake Nyanza, and so with Uganda, and by our shadowy White Nile Sphere of Influence,

AFRICA

with Egypt. By a Convention which ceded the colony of Heligoland to Germany, and is known as the Convention of July, 1890, relating to Africa and Heligoland, Germany was brought by Lord Salisbury to Lake Tanganyika and Lake Victoria Nyanza, and to join the Congo State on a common frontier between those two lakes near what was formerly called the Stevenson Road,—thus blocking out Mr. Rhodes from the accomplishment of his Cape to Cairo project. Lord Rosebery and Lord Kimberley afterwards attempted to lease a strip from the Congo State, which would have given us, subject to the terms of this lease, an All-British road; but the Germans interfered in a most unfriendly fashion and forced the Congo State to destroy this Convention. It is hard to see how, except by the mere leave of Germany, or of the Congo State, Mr. Rhodes can hope to pass from British Central Africa to British Uganda.

These difficulties of South and Central Africa offer little or no present risk of war.

THE BRITISH EMPIRE

But the same could not till lately be said of the difficulties on the West, nor can it be said of those further north. The British East Africa Protectorate has no northern frontier. We came to an understanding with Italy for a common frontier as far as Italy was concerned, but the Italians have been driven by Abyssinia from the greater portion of their sphere, and our own recent treaty with the Emperor Menelik of Ethiopia has not established even a *modus vivendi* between us and him on this, the more difficult and the more important, as well as by far the longest, portion of our common frontier. According to the colouring of British maps, British East Africa reaches to a British sphere composed of the former Equatorial Provinces of Egypt. But our pretensions to this sphere are ridiculed by some of the other Powers. A portion of it indeed is now occupied by the Congo State under lease from us, and this lease has been recognized by France and may be looked upon as solidly established: but north of this again

AFRICA

a French expedition has seated itself upon the streams flowing down into the Nile in one of the Equatorial Provinces of Egypt now coloured pink upon our maps, and the French assert that they have as good a right to be there in the name of Egypt as we possibly can have. Moreover, we are not there and never have been. From the north the Egyptian Sirdar* is pressing southwards, with British troops added to his Egyptian forces, for the purpose of reasserting the authority of the Khedive as against the Dervishes. If on the arrival of his steamers on the White Nile, he finds the French seated upon that river, it is difficult to see how a European Conference is to be avoided, or to prophesy what the outcome of that Conference may be. If, on the other hand, the French expedition is not more strongly established than we suppose, it will probably find it necessary to retire before the flying bands of Dervishes, dispersed by General Kitchener, and we shall possibly then

* Written in July, 1898.

discover that the Marchand and Liotard expeditions are "private expeditions," paid for out of the funds of the French colonial party, although exclusively officered by officers of that admirable force the *Infanterie de la Marine et des Colonies*, commonly known in France as "the Dog Fish."

The marvellous activity of the French has brought them into conflict with us not only as regards the country south-west of Khartoum, but as regards the back country of Lagos and of the Gold Coast: the back country of our other two colonies is already gone,—swallowed up by France beyond return. Starting from the West Coast, the French, with extraordinary vigour, have penetrated south-east to the Lower Niger, and due east almost to the Nile. Marvellous as have been our own exploits in all parts of the world, we can hardly show any enterprise to compare with that of the French colonial forces. The future of our Niger sphere must be important, but it hardly looks as though, in face of French development, it could ever lead to the foundation of an African empire in the least comparable to our Indian Empire. The probability is that the expectations which have been formed with regard to the future of Africa will be a disappointment to all the Powers concerned. The Germans have hopelessly failed to make much of their three chief colonies, and the French have been pouring out money and French life like water without much hope of a tangible return. The Congo State is beginning to make money, but by a system of government (if such a name can be applied to it) so ruthless and extortionate that we have some ground for congratulation that, whatever may be alleged against our rule in parts of Africa, we at all events are far less bad than our Belgian rivals. While, then, I look forward to a great development of trade in our Niger sphere and to some possible development of stock-farming in a portion of the high country which lies to the west of the British East Africa Protectorate, and

THE BRITISH EMPIRE

to the east of Uganda, as well as to a steady development of British South Africa, I cannot profess to believe that any other portion of Africa is likely to show the material prosperity which has been attained by the marvellously-fertile irrigated strip along the Nile which forms the Khediviate of Egypt.

The future of Africa unfortunately can hardly be contemplated without the expectation of eventual war. The divisions which the recent partition of Africa among the Powers has brought about are too purely artificial to survive in a great war where the command of the sea is seriously disputed between ourselves and a Coalition. The future of Africa will one day be settled, but that future is never likely to produce such spheres of trade as those which India and which South America present.

CHAPTER VIII

CROWN COLONIES

THE present position of our Crown Colonies in general connects itself with that of those situate on the West Coast of Africa, and in the northern portions of South Africa, which have been mentioned. If it is right to pour out money in Africa as the mother-country has been pouring it out for some time past (a question with regard to which I have grave doubts), it would seem also to be wise to expend money in developing some of our backward Crown Colonies of high fertility which are pining for capital in other portions of the world. If it is worth spending five millions upon a railroad leading to

Uganda, it might be worth spending a quarter of a million in the development of the back country of British Guiana, which is probably of far greater value than Uganda or any of the countries in the neighbourhood of Uganda. If we cannot make the most fertile of the West India Islands pay, how can we expect to make countries which are less healthy and far less fertile, in the very heart of Africa, return a profit? Our people have been interested in Africa through their traditional desire to suppress the evils of the slave trade, and to pay conscience money in these days for the sins, in connection with slavery, of their predecessors; but it is probable that we have done more harm by promoting the partition of Africa and the creation, in the name of liberty, of such governments as that of the Congo Free State, than the harm which our grandfathers did to Africa by their participation in African slavery and the slave trade. There is no one who knows both Africa and India so well as Dr. Cust,

CROWN COLONIES

formerly connected with the Indian Government, with the Royal Asiatic Society, and with the Church Missionary Society. He has pronounced a confident opinion—defended out of the vast stores of his learning—that the greater part of Africa will never pay, and that we have no prospect of establishing in the heart of that vast country such a government as we have, to our glory, set up in India. When we turn to our Crown Colonies and Dependencies in other portions of the world we shall find that they present a different picture, and one which, in spite of depression in the West Indies, we can contemplate with pride.

We may include under the general heading "Crown Colonies" both Crown Colonies proper—wholly governed from home—and colonies possessing institutions which are representative though not responsible. It is easier to class the colonies by the purposes for which they are maintained, and which they chiefly serve, than to group them according to their systems of government.

THE BRITISH EMPIRE

Gibraltar, Malta, Cyprus (which is nominally only leased to us and remains Turkish soil), the Falklands, and Bermuda, with some others, are mainly coaling stations or naval bases; Cyprus being indeed useless for such purposes, but having been foolishly occupied from the same point of view as that from which Gibraltar and Malta were conquered and have been held. Hong Kong is a military station and a naval base, but it is also in a high degree a trading station,—in part, it is to be feared, like Gibraltar, a smuggling station. The Straits, so far as their chief port, Singapore, is concerned, are a naval base and a coaling station and a great distributing entrepôt of trade; but contain within one government Protectorates in the Malay Peninsula which are of high value from the plantation and the mining point of view. Not far off, in the Archipelago, we have Borneo, where similar wealth—likely to become important as regards the future in the case of tobacco —exists to that found in the Malay Protected

States. British Borneo is worth special notice on account of curiosities of government.

The rise in modern times of the Chartered Companies, of which the Imperial British East Africa Company sold to the Government its territorial rights, and of which the Niger Company and the British South Africa Company have been mentioned in the last chapter, commenced with the grant by Mr. Gladstone's second Administration of the Charter to the British North Borneo Company. That grant was supported by Lord Granville, who was a "Cobdenite," if not what is now called a "Little Englander," and by Mr. Gladstone, who, on the 17th March, 1882, laid down in the House of Commons the doctrine that the grant of the charter was in limitation of those general and larger rights which British subjects would otherwise have possessed without any charter from the Crown at all. Considering, however, that the grant of the Charter in the case of all these companies—and the three African charters closely followed the lines of the British North Borneo Charter—was that which gave their chief value to their shares, Mr. Gladstone's doctrine can hardly be defended by ordinary men. The grant of charters seems to have been a half-way house towards the greater colonial activity which is now popular, and if such activity is wise it is probably more wise when conducted directly by the Colonial Office than when conducted by companies for profit. The history of the Hudson Bay Company, and that of the East India Company, is, on the whole, not inglorious. But these companies were pretty closely watched by Parliament, and they existed in times when the newspaper press was not the power which it is in the present day. The experience which we have had of Chartered Companies in recent times goes to show that their life will be short, and that Governments may be compelled to buy them out at a price which will represent more than the cost of founding British Government in the

CROWN COLONIES

territories in question had this task been directly undertaken by the Colonial Office. In the case of British North Borneo, the former colony of Labuan has now been virtually attached to the government of the Chartered Company. There should also be mentioned in this connection the neighbouring protected native Sultanate of Brunei and the protected kingdom of Sarawak of which the Rajah is an Englishman.

The greatest of our recent successes in the government of tropical dependencies is that which has been exhibited in the case of Ceylon. The apparent downfall of that beautiful colony in consequence of the coffee disease, and its marvellous restoration by the enterprise of the British planters, with the result of the virtual suppression of the China tea trade to the United Kingdom by the Ceylon tea interest, present one of those pictures of the ups and downs of the life of a young country which are as interesting to some observers as the scenery of our tropical colonies to others.

THE BRITISH EMPIRE

Another pleasant picture is that presented by Mauritius, a colony in which we rule by French institutions, what may be described as a French people—as French in their way as are the inhabitants of the province of Quebec. The inhabitants of Mauritius are partly the descendants of French aristocratic colonists, partly French "coloured" people of the various shades of a mixed race. In the Ile de France, as Mauritius was called during the longer portion of her history, there was no native population. She appears literally to have risen from the seas, and the skeleton of the dodo alone recalls a native race. The French were there, with their negroes, from 1715 for nearly one hundred years, and were firmly rooted in the island. We have introduced a large number of Indian labourers, but three-fourths of the population are still nominally Roman Catholic, and a great many of them pretty fiercely French, and even French-republican, in sentiment, though not disloyal to our rule, on account of the continued existence of

CROWN COLONIES

French institutions, including the *Code civil*, and the care which the Colonial Office has on the whole shown of their prejudices as well as of their interests. It is worth noting that, although Mauritius depends almost entirely upon sugar, her trade statistics are not of that gloomy description which West Indian comments on the state of the sugar industry would prepare us to expect.

Fiji, in the centre of the Pacific, is also a sugar colony, and here again sugar appears to maintain itself without suffering heavily as in the West Indies it has suffered—it is alleged—owing to the operation of the bounty-system.

The great group of colonies consisting of British Honduras—with its mahogany, logwood, and other forest wealth,—of British Guiana—with its Demerara sugar and its gold,—and of the West Indies—with their sugar, their cocoa, and their increasing fruit trade to the United States,—has not in these days the relative importance which it possessed in the colonial world of the early portion of the century. The Bahamas and some of our other islands are becoming tourist fields of American travel; but the future of the West Indies is somewhat dark, inasmuch as the contiguity of the United States, and the desire of the United States from time to time to make modifications of tariff, with a view to bringing the British West Indies more and more within their orbit and of exercising pressure upon them, are disturbing circumstances.

Nothing can rob the British West Indies of their lovely scenery, which will undoubtedly attract an increasing number of visitors to them, as the world becomes more populous, more rich, and more dull,—given the fact that their climate is healthy for a climate of the tropics. On the other hand, nothing seems likely to confer on our West Indian colonies the blessing of as enterprising a population of planters as that with which Ceylon or Northern Queensland presents us. The curse of negro slavery still hangs about the islands, and the fostering care which was

CROWN COLONIES

at one time extended by the State towards their commercial growth has in the long run damaged the commercial efficiency of local capital and produced results which now prevent the flow of capital from the mother-country to these colonies. The West Indies are connected with some of the grandest military exploits of our history. The Carib Sea was the cradle of the British Navy, and the scene not only of the exploits of Raleigh and of Drake, but of those of the pirates under Morgan. The brave deeds of the buccaneers, ultimately suppressed by us, were rivalled by those of Blake, under the Commonwealth, and of Rodney, Hood, and Nelson in later times. Our Atlantic colonies now differ greatly among themselves. As has been shown in an admirable paper by Mr. Carrington, while Barbadoes and some others are intensely English, even the pure negro population being thoroughly Anglicised, others of the islands, such as Dominica, St. Lucia, and Grenada, still show signs of French possession, not so striking as those displayed by Mauritius, but sufficient to make it difficult to apply to them exactly the same system of government as that for which Barbadoes is prepared. Trinidad, too, retains a Spanish element, and British Guiana a Dutch. So close must commercial relations between the United States and the West Indies be, that there are many Britons in the West Indies who are inclined, under the depression produced by the decline of profits in the sugar industry, almost to welcome a faint prospect of eventual American sovereignty in the islands. On the other hand, if the Isthmus Canal should ever be completed, St. Lucia as our naval base will become of considerable military importance. It is not probable that the British Parliament, under any condition of affairs that can be foreseen, is likely to accept a transfer of sovereignty in the islands, to which the negro and "coloured" majority of the population would be bitterly opposed.

Apart from sugar the West Indies may yet have a commercial future. Grenada now grows cacao, Jamaica fruit and tobacco, on an increasing scale. The substitution of new industries for those connected with sugar tends to assist the growth of a negro peasant proprietary, which has already come into existence in Jamaica.

It is difficult to pick out the sugar industry for special artificial treatment, as it is by no means the only colonial industry which is harmed by foreign bounties. Newfoundland, for example, finds its fish trade greatly hampered by French law, and has, under all the circumstances of the case, a stronger claim for special and exceptional treatment than have even the West Indies.

Personally I cannot but think that the experiment which has been tried by France in Martinique and Guadaloupe,—of promoting peasant proprietary and of giving the negroes and the coloured people a constantly increasing share in the government of the colonies, in which they form the overwhelming majority of the population,—will sooner or later have to be adopted in the

THE BRITISH EMPIRE

British West Indies. The West Indian coloured people are by no means to be despised as regards the power of government which they have already shown. Some of the most distinguished officials of the islands, even under the present somewhat oligarchic system of government, belong to the coloured race, and it is difficult to believe that the result of the long training which we have given to the West Indian "coloured" people and even to the negroes, cannot now justify the extension to them of a larger share in the government of the islands than is yet theirs.

CHAPTER IX

IMPERIAL DEFENCE

THE defence of the colonies of the British Empire must rest mainly upon our naval supremacy, which is also necessary, however, both for the protection of India and of the mother-country against invasion, and for the maintenance of our trade.

Our naval supremacy at the present moment is more complete than it has been in the recent past; but it is, owing to the efforts of our rivals, unhappily more complete now than it is likely to be in the immediate future. 1898 is a year in which we stand in a strong position, especially so far as battleships are concerned, by the completion of the *Magnificent* class of the

Spencer programme, and by the non-completion of the corresponding ships of the other Powers. It is, however, unfortunately the case that Mr. T. A. Brassey, who has hitherto been looked upon by many of us as an optimist, explains in the most important chapters of the *Naval Annual*, published in April last, that we are about to again lose our advantage as compared even with the Franco-Russian combination. It is pointed out, in the valuable Russian chapter of that work, that Russia is now building, even as compared with ourselves, with "unexampled rapidity," and that while she has until now been obliged to buy armour plating from abroad, she will very soon be able to herself supply all the armour needed for her immense new programme, fully revealed only in the month of May. As regards the manning of our ships, Mr. T. A. Brassey, who had formerly appeared to be fairly satisfied, now declares that our "numbers" may "without hesitation" be declared "insufficient."

IMPERIAL DEFENCE

I have recently pressed on the attention of the Admiralty a suggestion which had previously been made, by Mr. Brassey among others, that colonial assistance towards increase of numbers might with advantage be sought by us. But I have limited myself to advising an experiment in this direction in the colony of Newfoundland. In Australasia the numbers of fishermen and coasting seamen are small and their pay is high. As regards Canada there is a danger that if the local fishermen are trained they will be attracted by high bounties into the navy of the United States, instead of being available for our own. In the case of Newfoundland alone is there an immense supply of hardy fishermen and sailors, working at low rates of pay, and, therefore, probably willing to accept the rates offered for the new home Reserve, while at the same time sufficiently (geographically) removed from the temptations of the United States to be probably available in time of war.

Direct colonial contribution towards Imperial defence is a matter which needs discussion. At the present moment Canada, with her long frontier, assists in the defence of the naval base of Esquimalt, at one end of it, and does not assist in the defence of the fortified base of Halifax at the other end. Halifax, however, would probably be retained by us as a coaling station in any event, just as we retain the fortified station of Bermuda. Canada supplies, under a nominal system of universal militia service, a small permanent militia of decreasing strength, supported as regards its officering by an admirable Staff College. The supply of artillery and of ammunition of a modern type, as well as that of rifles, is insufficient for the strain of war; but war between ourselves and the United States is not to be expected, and the United States have also not hitherto maintained upon the Canadian frontier any permanent force. Canada makes no contribution towards the fleet, which, however, defends for her a large

IMPERIAL DEFENCE

portion of her frontier, owing to the navigability of the St. Lawrence. The Australasian colonies maintain a considerable militia force of various types, besides a large number of volunteers, and they contribute towards the maintenance of a local squadron, which is subject to a condition of irremovability which would greatly hamper the Admiralty in time of war, and which, although wholly indefensible on strategical grounds, is one which the Prime Ministers of the colonies insist on maintaining—against the best advice. The South African colonies have shown signs of a willingness to contribute towards the fleet, and they maintain a considerable local military force, besides accepting a universal liability to the call to arms, which they have inherited from the Dutch Colonial Government. The Crown Colonies contribute towards the cost of the army, but upon a low, although a varying, scale. It is difficult to see why Ceylon and Singapore, with their enormous trade, should contribute towards the defence of the Empire on a scale far lower than that which applies to the south of India, which is less exposed to attack, as well as far poorer from every point of view.

When we look round the Empire as a whole we cannot but be struck by the want of system which prevails, and the haphazard fashion in which the subject has always been treated by Governments at home. We have indeed made little progress with regard to the principle upon which it should be dealt with. Even before the commencement of the eighteenth century Penn made proposals for an Imperial Congress, or at least an American Congress, to be presided over by a Commissioner from home, which was to decide on the contributions to be made by the different colonies for the purpose of Imperial Defence. During the great wars with France in the eighteenth century the colonial troops played the grandest part; and, as Mr. Hugh Egerton has pointed out, if real statesmanship had been exhibited at

IMPERIAL DEFENCE

that time, "It might have been possible to attach to the service of the Crown a colonial army, which might have rendered the immediate course of history very different. . . . The presence of a loyal American army might have been a force, making for British interests, the importance of which could not be exaggerated. So far was the British Government from attempting this that by a most unwise regulation all commissions in the Royal army above the rank of Captain took precedence of all commissions in the Colonial service."

It is often thought that the American colonies rose against the very principle of taxation for Imperial purposes considered in the abstract. But, as Mr. Egerton has well shown, Franklin himself, writing in 1764, admitted that a special revenue might properly be established towards supporting troops to be maintained in America by the Crown, and the principle that the colonists should pay their due proportion of Imperial charges was not denied by the colonists themselves; their grievance lying wholly in the particular manner in which payment was required.

It will perhaps be sufficient for our purpose here if we simply note the fact that the most fanatically independent and self-contained of all our colonies, those most disposed to resist inclusion with ourselves in a common government under any scheme of Imperial Federation, would, undoubtedly, in the judgment of those who know them best, be anxious to take their part in defending the Empire;—for example, in India in time of dangerous war against a coalition. This being so, surely it must be wise that such preparation for collective action should be made in time of peace as would come too late if postponed till time of war.

CHAPTER X

CONCLUSION

In his speech at Birmingham on the 13th May, the Colonial Secretary, after explaining the dangers which surround our position as a Power, expressed the desire of himself and the Cabinet to draw closer the bonds between ourselves and our colonies for the purposes of defence and of trade. No proposals have, however, as yet been put forward for consideration upon the former head, and those which have been suggested upon the latter have either been withdrawn or are somewhat nebulous.

The Colonial Secretary, who, before the Jubilee, invited practical suggestions for a tariff union, after he had met the Prime

Ministers of the eleven self-governing colonies, declared in strong terms the unwisdom of pressing the question. But since that declaration steps have been taken in some colonies in the direction of a preference to be given to the produce and manufactures of the United Kingdom. It will be seen that the phrase "the United Kingdom" excludes India and the Crown Colonies, and it is by no means certain that any very real or considerable preference can be carried, as far as the United Kingdom itself is concerned, in the Protectionist colonies; while colonies which are not Protectionist will rather desire to open more freely their gates than to open them specially to the mother-country. It is mainly against the manufactures of Great Britain and the wheat of India that the colonial Protectionists direct their doctrine. The cheap-living Asiatic populations, and the "pauper labour," which excite their scorn, inhabit above all British India.

CONCLUSION

The only practical step which is being taken at the present time with regard to increased trade facilities concerns a renewal of reciprocity arrangements between the West Indies (British Crown Colonies) and a foreign country—the United States. Already there is a partial customs-union between British colonies and a foreign country—the Orange Free State. There was previously a reciprocity treaty between Canada and the United States, and there may be again. It is indeed somewhat doubtful whether the vision of a British tariff league is less of a dream-vision than that of absolute Imperial unity or federation. We shall all agree on one point, which is that it is unwise to press any proposals for change which will provoke in any considerable portions of the Empire resistance likely to worsen the existing state of feeling, and this may be the effect of pressing freer admission of British goods upon Protectionist colonies, or closer political relations upon others.

THE BRITISH EMPIRE

Even from the point of view of British power and authority in the world, and from the point of view of peace, most necessary to British trade, it is doubtful whether the drawing closer of commercial bonds within the Empire, at the expense of commercial relations with other countries, is a step of progress. Take Canada, for example. Canada and the United States are so situate towards one another that their trade, except for artificial and political but imaginary lines, would be chiefly with one another. Not only in the days of Reciprocity, but up to June, 1896, the trade of the United States with Canada was very large indeed. The hostile tariff of the United States has harmed this trade, and has caused the action on the part of Sir Wilfrid Laurier which excited much attention last year, but these steps are less natural and more strained than would be a complete or even partial removal of customs barriers between Canada and her nearer neighbour; while the political

CONCLUSION

estrangement which commercial estrangement brings about is not to the advantage either of our Imperial policy or of peace. The sentiment of common nationality and of racial patriotism, which it is undoubtedly important to strengthen within our Empire, may be called out by a wise policy of common Imperial defence, without being accompanied by an attempt to divert trade by steps which could not fail in some degree to hamper that European trade and that trade to the Two Americas upon which statistics show that our manufacturing supremacy and overwhelming maritime supremacy depend. Attempts to divert trade for the supposed benefit of the colonies, or of the mother-country in connection with her colonial Empire, are, of course, not new. They constitute a milder form of that Colonial System which was formerly applied in a greater or less degree by the countries possessing colonies, and which in its extreme form excluded from the ports of such countries and their colonies all foreign ships and all foreign goods.

Those who are interested in the details of the fiscal question which is involved in proposals either for a Zollverein or for preferential trade within the Empire, or parts of it, would do well to study for themselves Mr. Chamberlain's speech upon the subject delivered on the 25th March, 1896, at a meeting of the Canada Club. It has been commonly assumed by partisans that Mr. Chamberlain proclaimed on that occasion a policy different from that which had been the policy of the Colonial Office and of British Cabinets in the past. He stated, on the contrary, the objections to the proposal of the majority of the Colonial representatives at the Ottawa Conference of 1894 (presided over with singular statesmanship by Lord Jersey) in the strongest terms. He said that preferential trade would involve, in the case of the United Kingdom, a most serious disturbance of our trade, the imposition of a duty upon food

CONCLUSION

and upon raw material, with a tendency to increase the cost of living, to increase the pressure upon the working classes of this country, to increase the cost of production, and to put us in a worse position in competition with foreign countries in neutral markets. All this for an insufficient *quid pro quo*. He showed that our foreign trade is so gigantic in proportion to the foreign trade of our colonies that the burden of any arrangement of the kind would fall with great weight on the home country. He stated that Lord Ripon's despatch of 1895 was conclusive against the particular proposal which up to 1896 had been suggested for our consideration. But he pointed out that Lord Ripon himself had alluded to a different proposal which had not been made, which would be free in principle from objection, and which, if practicable, would cement the unity of the Empire and promote its progress. This was a proposal for a true Zollverein, but since that time the total

THE BRITISH EMPIRE

unwillingness of every colony to come into such an arrangement has been demonstrated; so that it is at present unnecessary to discuss the objections which, in spite of Lord Ripon's words, torn from their context, would undoubtedly remain to any such proposal.

In a speech of the 9th June, 1896, Mr. Chamberlain returned to the subject and spoke more strongly still in favour of the establishment of commercial union throughout the Empire, but admitted that it would involve the replacing (by the mother-country) of duties upon corn, meat, wool, and other articles of enormous consumption in this country. He did not think it either wise or practicable that any such proposal should come in the first instance from the United Kingdom; and a sufficient answer, for the moment, is that no such proposal has come from the colonies. One enormous difficulty in the way of even fairly considering such proposals, should they be made at

CONCLUSION

a future time, is that of how to represent the interests of India, containing as she does the majority of British subjects in the world, and supplying as she does an enormous share of the income and of the military resources of the Empire. Mr. Chamberlain's suggestion met with what the leading newspapers in Australia describe as a "cool reception," and the fate of "falling flat," and the final blow was given to it when the eleven Prime Ministers of the self-governing colonies met at the Colonial Office during the Jubilee. It must never be forgotten in this connection that, even under hostile tariffs, the first of our export markets continues to be the United States; while the second of our export markets is the vast Empire of India, under our rule indeed, but too little thought of in connection with this matter of colonial tariffs and colonial trade.

There is a danger in pressing Imperial Federation, without knowing exactly what we mean and, still more, what the colonies desire. There is danger in pressing closer trade relations while we remain in the same condition of doubt. There is danger in neglecting to press those joint preparations for Imperial Defence which, if not made now, will come too late.

CHAPTER XI

HOW TO STUDY THE EMPIRE [*]

I HAVE been asked for a short article on "How to Study the Empire;" and, wasting no space on introduction, will divide the subject into—How the Empire has Grown Up; and What It is Now. On the history of the British Empire I would, in the strongest manner, recommend Mr. Hugh Egerton's "Colonial Policy." The lighter Elizabethan literature will, in some cases, be found referred to in Mr. Egerton's notes; but I would mention as specially worthy of attention all that bears on Sir Walter Raleigh's voyages and life. Sir J. Seeley's "Expansion of England" is excellent with

[*] Reprinted by kind permission from the Literary Supplement of the *Critic*, Nov. 5, 1898.

regard to the wars of the last century and the philosophical and historical positions which underlay and survived them.

With regard to the present position of the Empire, dealing first with generalities, I would name Escott's "England," Dr. Todd's "Parliamentary Government in the Colonies," and "The Great Alternative" and "The Nation's Awakening," by Mr. Spenser Wilkinson. For reference, there should always be at hand "The Statesman's Year-Book," a good atlas and also a large globe. The exclusive use of the atlas, without constant reference to the globe, is a snare of the first order. The relative magnitude of various countries, and their position in relation to one another, are continually lost sight of. The "projections" of "The World" maps avoid only the former of these two difficulties.

When we come to the study of particular parts of the Empire, I would recommend for India Sir W. Hunter's "Indian Empire," Sir G. Chesney's "Indian Polity"; and,

HOW TO STUDY THE EMPIRE

above all, the annual Blue Book called a "Report on the Moral and Material Progress of India," which is published generally about the end of July; and the last number of which was circulated to Members of both Houses of Parliament and placed on sale early in August last.

For the Dominion of Canada, I would advise the reading of Bourinot's "Canada" and of Dawson's "North America" in Stanford's Compendium. All the volumes of this geographical work are good; but the North American volume stands high as an authority. It includes Newfoundland, which is, of course, outside the Dominion, and on which there should also be studied the various books of the Reverend Dr. M. Harvey.

For Australia, the book of the late Dr. Dale is excellent. My own "Problems of Greater Britain" is a work now somewhat out of date, but hardly yet wholly superseded in its Australian portions. Mr. Walker's book, which has recently appeared,

THE BRITISH EMPIRE

is good, but far from full. It should be seen, as should, for Australian political philosophy, "The Law of the Constitution of South Australia," by Mr. Blackmore, the Clerk of Parliaments of that Colony, who was also Clerk to the recent Commonwealth Convention, of which the "Hansard" should be studied. If the Australian "Hansard" were as heavy as our own and as full of undigested matter, I should hesitate to recommend it. But the Commonwealth Convention was composed of picked men, and some of the debates—notably those of March 11 of the present year on the provisions for a deadlock between the two Houses, and of March 18 on the Commonwealth Bill as a whole—are at a far higher average level than are the debates in the Imperial Parliament. Those who desire to acquaint themselves with the lives of the statesmen of Australia and New Zealand will find them recorded in Mr. Philip Mennell's "Dictionary of Australasian Biography." For light literature Mrs.

HOW TO STUDY THE EMPIRE

Campbell Praed's "Australian Life," and, indeed, her Queensland novels, may be recommended; as well as "Uncle Piper of Piper's Hill," by the lady who wrote under the name of "Tasma,"—the late Madame Couvreur, the *Times*' correspondent at Brussels.

New Zealand has a large literature, from which I would select, for the former state of things, "Old New Zealand," by "A Pakeha Maori"; and the New Zealand chapters of my own "Greater Britain"—the only part of that book, in the author's opinion, now worth reading, so greatly have things changed since 1868, when it was published, or 1866–7, when it was written. For the present state of things in New Zealand the best thing to see is a little book in "The Story of the Empire" Series by the Hon. W. P. Reeves, the present Agent-General and late Minister for Labour, or his "The Long White Cloud; Ao Tea Roa."

For South Africa I should advise the reading of Greswell's "Our South African

THE BRITISH EMPIRE

Empire" and of Keane's "South Africa," in Stanford's Compendium. The greatest of Colonial novels belongs to British South Africa—Olive Schreiner's "African Farm."

If it is thought that I have picked out, on the whole, a somewhat serious class of volume, I must throw the responsibility upon the Editor; because, in his letter, although he alludes to reading for "young" Englishmen, he refers to "study" of the Empire. The young generally choose their light literature for themselves; but, of course, Elizabethan adventure and early American adventure are largely represented in the favourite light literature of the day, as are the fortunes of the British Navy. The question as put to me by the Editor hardly includes political discussion of the future of the Empire. It may, however, be worth adding that the best things that have been penned upon the side of Imperial Federation are the writings of Mr. Parkin. I, myself, have always inclined to caution in this matter, for the reasons which I have

HOW TO STUDY THE EMPIRE

stated in Part VII. of "Problems of Greater Britain," which deals with "Future Relations between the Mother Country and the Remainder of the Empire."

By way of summary let me recommend those who do not desire so large a body of reading as I have suggested, to turn to Mr. Hugh Egerton's "Colonial Policy," first named; and to the books of Mr. Spenser Wilkinson.

ST. PIERRE AND MIQUELON

Note on words used at p. 48 which may be misunderstood.

THE Rev. M. Harvey, and a more recent writer in his *The Tenth Island*, are unfortunately wrong in thinking that we can now stand on the letter of any Treaty or on the words of the Treaty of 1763, and in view of their statements my own words need explanation. It must be remembered that the islands after their cession in 1763 were again taken by us, and again ceded (in 1783). On the latter occasion the words of the Treaty of 1763 were not repeated, and the naked cession of the islands was one of the grounds on which Lord Shelburne's ministry was upset by Fox and others, and a vote of censure on them, for concluding the Treaty, carried in the House of Commons. Had the approval of the Treaty by Parliament been necessary under the constitution of this country, it would not have been obtained. St. Pierre and Miquelon, in the 103 years from 1713 to 1816, were for seventy-eight years British, and for only twenty-five years French; fifteen of these years under the Treaty of 1763. During the other ten years the French acted on the spirit of the French King's declaration, which is the subject of my remarks on p. 49. If we are in any degree to uphold the spirit of our own King's declaration and to go, as we have always gone, beyond the letter of the Treaties, it is obvious that we ought to resent any violation of the spirit of the French King's declaration, and of his acceptance of the principles laid down in the declaration of His Britannic Majesty. By our own declaration, accepted by the French, the islands were to be a "shelter" for their fishermen. The French King, in his declaration, ridiculed the notion that trouble could arise out of his occupation for this purpose of the two islands. But my belief, that fortification of St. Pierre and Miquelon is a violation of the Declarations, is contrary to the opinion entertained at the time, and I must not press it.

INDEX

A

ADEN, portion of Presidency of Bombay, 16
Africa, 100
    Colonies in, various governments, 102
    Colonies of West Coast, 101, 113
    French activity in, 100
    Future prospects of, 111
    West Africa Frontier Force, 12
    (*See* British Central Africa Protectorate, British East Africa, etc.)
Agra—
    pearl mosque of, 31
    Taj, the, 31
Algeria, Government of, 7
Alsace, attitude of inhabitants towards France, 40
Ameer of Afghanistan a popular ruler, 26
American Colonies and taxation for Imperial purposes, 133
Ascension, Island of, under the Admiralty, 16, 102

Australasia—
    Federal Council, 71, 74
    Militia, 131
    Position of, 6
Australia—
    and British power, 70
    Books recommended on, 147, 148
    Commonwealth Bill, 72, 76, 84
    Western, attitude towards Commonwealth Bill, 80, 83
Australian Colonies, attitude towards maintenance of British fleet, 45
Australian Colonies local fleet, 12
Author (Sir Charles Dilke)—
    Adult Suffrage Bill, 94
    On Newfoundland Act (1891), 60

B

Ballance Administration, New Zealand, 88
Barbadoes, 123
Barton and Federal Protectionists, 82

INDEX

Bermuda, 130
Bolan Pass, 17
Brassey, Hon. T. A., on British Navy, 128
British Borneo, Curiosities of Government, 117
British Central Africa Protectorate, 103
British Colonies (*see* Colonies)
British Columbia, minerals in, 45
British East Africa—
    Foreign Office army in, 12
    Protectorate, no northern frontier, 108
British Empire—
    Area, population, revenue, 1
    Books recommended on, 145, 146
    Component parts of, 6
    Goldfields, 2
    Influence of laws and race, 5
    Naval Supremacy, 12
    Productions, 2
    Schemes for closer union, 11, 143
British Guiana, development of, 114, 121
British Honduras, 121
British Naval Supremacy, 127
British New Zealander, characteristics, 98
British North Borneo Company, 117, 119
British rule in India uniform, 21
British Somaliland under Aden, 16
British South Africa Company, 117
Brunei, Sultanate of, 119

C

California, discovery of surface gold in, 44
Canada—
    Books recommended on, 147
    Decrease of friction between Roman Catholics and Protestants in, 42
    Defence of Naval base of Esquimalt, 130
    Military service in, 43
    Mineral wealth, 35, 44
    Roman Catholic Church in French Canada, 41
    Territory and resources, 5
    Two dominant peoples in, 33
    United Empire Loyalists in, 33
Canada and United States, trade between, 137, 138
Cape Colony, 104
    Governor of, his powers, 100
    Mainly Dutch, 104
    Offer of ironclad, 13
Cape of Good Hope, 16
Carib Sea, cradle of British Navy, 123
Central Africa Protectorate, Foreign Office army in, 12
Ceylon—
    Coffee and tea trade of, 119
    Contribution to defence of Empire, 131
    Government of, 15
Chamberlain, Right Hon. J.—
    On tariff union with Colonies, 135

INDEX

Chamberlain, Rt. Hn. J.—*contd.*
   Speech at Canada Club, 140
   Speech on commercial union throughout Empire, 140, 142
Chartered companies, 117
Churchill, Lord Randolph, increases white army in India, 20
Colonial Office military forces, 12
Colonies—
   Defence of, 127, 129
   Government of, 6, 15
   (*See* also Crown Colonies and different titles)
Commonwealth of Australia Bill (1897-1898), 72, 76, 84
   And Senate, 82
Congo State, 107, 108, 111
   Government of, 114
Crown Colonies, 113 *seqq.*
   Contribute to cost of army, 131
   Forms of government, 15
Cust, Dr., on prospects of African Colonies, 114
Cyprus, 116; government of, 17

D

Dawson, S. E., 147
Delhi, pearl mosque of, 31
Dominion of Canada (*see* Canada)
Drake, Sir Francis, 123

E

East India Company, 118
Egerton, Hugh—
   "Colonial Policy," 145, 151
   On British Empire, 8

Egerton, Hugh—*continued*
   On Colonial troops, 132
   On "Greater Britain," 9
   Quotes Montcalm on loss of Canada, 70
Empress of India, 14
Escott, J. H. S., 146
Esquimalt, 43, 130

F

Falkland Isles, 116
Federal Council of Australasia, 71, 74
Figaro rendering of Greater Britain, 10
Fiji, Crown Colony, 71
   and Federal Council of Australasia, 71
   Government of, 15
   Sugar colony, 3, 121
Flourens, M., on "French Shore," Newfoundland, 66
Foreign Office armies in British East Africa, Uganda, etc., 12
Forrest, Sir John, on Commonwealth Bill, 80
France, relations with England in Africa, 101
Franklin on special revenue for support of troops in America, 133
Free Traders in Australasia, 84
French activity in Africa, 110
French Canadians, attitude towards Great Britain, 36, 39
French Colonies, 3; cost of, 7, 8
French Soudan, 7
French, the, and Newfoundland, 46 *seqq.*

INDEX

G

German Colonies, 3, 8; in Africa, 111
Gibraltar, why held, 6, 116
Gladstone, W. E., and British North Borneo Company, 117
Governor of Cape, his powers, 100
Granville, Earl, and British North Borneo Company, 117
Greater Britain, first use of term, 9
Grey, Sir George, Prime Minister of New Zealand, 88
Guadaloupe, French system of government, 125

H

Halifax, 43
    As coaling-station, 130
Harcourt, Sir William, Finance Bill, 78
Harvey, Hon. A. W., Newfoundland delegate to England, 49
Harvey, Rev. Dr. M., 147, 152
Heligoland ceded to Germany, 107
Hindoo and Mahommedan, religious feuds between, 25
Hofmeyr, proposal of British cable to Cape, 13
Hong Kong, government of, 17
Hudson Bay Company, 118
Hunter, Sir W. W., 146

I

Iddesleigh, Earl of, protests against erection of French lobster factories, 52

Ile de France (*see* Mauritius)
Imperial British East Africa Company, 117
Imperial Defence, 127 *seqq.*
    Preparations desirable for, 135, 144
Imperial Federation, danger in pressing, 137, 143
Imperial Service Troops in India, 20
India—
    and Nepal, 105
    British system of governing, 14, 18, 21, 27
    Compared with Russian Caucasus and Siberia, 8
    Condition (1898), 19
    Differences between districts, 25
    Drawback to British rule in, 23
    Feudatory states, government of, 20
    Finance, 19, 23, 28
    Impartiality of British rule not popular, 28
    Native police, 24, 28
    Native rulers' partiality popular, 28
    Native troops, 19
    Religious feuds, 25
    Scenery of, 31
    Theory of equality in, 29
    White Army in, 20
    (*See also* Native States)

J

Jamaica, industries of, 125
Jameson Raid, effect of, 104

INDEX

Jersey, Earl of, President of Ottawa Conference (1894), 140

K

Keane, A. H., 150
Kimberley, Earl of, attempt to lease strip from Congo State, 107
Kitchener, General, reasserting Khedive's authority, 109
Knutsford, Lord, on construction of French lobster factories, 53

L

Labouchere, Mr. (Secretary), and Newfoundland, 58, 59
Lagos under Colonial Office, 103
Lake Nyanza, 106
Lake Superior district, minerals in, 45
Lake Tanganyika, 106
Laurier, Sir Wilfrid—
    Action on tariff question, 138
    In Europe (1897), 45
Liotard Expedition, 109
Lobster-canning, Newfoundland, 53, 55

M

Madagascar, French action in, 46
Mahommedan and Hindoo, religious feuds between, 25
Malay Protected States, 116
Malta, why held, 6, 116
Maori women enfranchised, 95
Marchand Expedition, 109
Martens, de, librarian of Russian Foreign Office, 56
Martinique, French system of governing, 125
Mauritius (Ile de France)—
    Government of, 15
    History of, 120
    Sugar industry, 121
Menelik of Ethiopia, 108
Mennell, Philip, 148
Mill, J. S., Amendment on Disraeli's Reform Bill, 94
Miquelon ceded to France, 47, 152
Montcalm on loss of Canada, 70
Murray River, use of waters, 71
Mysore, Government of, 20, 25

N

Natal intensely British, 104
Native States (India)—
    As fields for administrative experiment, 30
    Diversity of, 21, 22
    Picturesqueness, 30
Negro slavery in West Indies, 122
New Guinea, 75
New South Wales and Federal Council of Australasia, 72, 75
New South Wales, vote on Commonwealth Bill, 73, 78
New Zealand—
    Aboriginal population, 87

INDEX

New Zealand—*continued*
    Adult suffrage, 87, 94
    Books recommended on, 149
    Compulsory Industrial Arbitration, 98
    Crown lands, 92
    Farm associations, 92
    Improved farm settlements, 93
    Inhabitants, characteristics, 98
    Labour legislation, 87, 91
    Life Insurance department of State, 98
    Natural beauty, 86
    "Old New Zealand" by a Pakeha Maori, 87, 149
    Prohibitionists and women voters, 96
    Public Trust Office, 98
    Radical and Labour Government, 88
    Shipping legislation, 91
    Unlike Australia, 90
    Variety of climate, 86
    Village settlements, 92
New Zealand and Federal Council of Australasia, 71
New Zealander, British, characteristics of, 98
Newfoundland—
    Cod-fisheries, 48, 55
    Fish-trade hampered by French law, 125
    "French Shore," 47, 50, 55, 61, 65
    Government, 50; attitude on lobster-fishing question, 57

Newfoundland—*continued*
    Lobster factories, 51 *seqq.*
    Men suitable for Naval Reserve in, 129
    Solicited to join Canadian Federation, 67
Newfoundland Act (fisheries), 60, 63
Newfoundland and France, 47
Niger, British sphere, development of, 111
Niger Company, 117; under Foreign Office, 103
Nile, White, sphere of influence, 101

O

Oil Rivers Protectorate under Foreign Office, 103
"Old New Zealand," by a Pakeha Maori, 87, 149
Ontario, discovery of gold, 45
Orange Free State, Dutch-Afrikander Republic, 105
    And British Colonies, partial customs-union between, 137
Ottawa Conference (1894), 140

P

Palmerston, Viscount, and Newfoundland, 58
Paris, Treaty of (1763), and Newfoundland, 47
Paris, Treaty of (1814), and Newfoundland, 49

INDEX

Parkin, G. R., 150
Penn, proposed Imperial Congress, 132
Protectionist Colonies and manufactures of Great Britain, 136

Q

Quebec, Province of, 39, 41
Queensland, attitude towards Commonwealth Bill, 80
Quetta, 17

R

Raleigh, Sir Walter, 123
Reeves, Hon. W. P., books on New Zealand, 88, 149
Reid, Right Hon. T., attitude towards Commonwealth Bill, 73, 74, 82
Rhodes, Right Hon. Cecil, projects in South Africa, 106
Ripon, Marquis of—
    Attitude on Newfoundland French lobster-fishing, 62, 63
    Despatch on foreign trade (1895), 141
Rosebery, Earl of, attempt to lease strip from Congo State, 107
Russia, dominions and position, 4
Russian Caucasus and Siberia compared with India, 8

S

St. Helena, 102
St. Lawrence River, 131
St. Lucia as coaling station, 124

St. Pierre ceded to France, 47, 152
Salisbury, Marquis of—
    Attitude on Newfoundland French lobster-fishing, 54, 60
    Convention of July, 1890, 107
Sarawak, protected kingdom, 119
Schreiner, Olive, 150
Seddon, Right Hon. R., and miners of South Island, New Zealand, 89
Siam, French in, 46
Singapore—
    Contribution to defence, 131
    Naval base, 116
Socotra, dependency of Aden, 102
Somaliland Protectorate, 102
Soudan, French, 7
South Africa, books recommended on, 149–50
South African Republic (*see* Transvaal)
South Australia—
    Adult Suffrage in, 81
    Vote on Commonwealth Bill, 72
Stanford's Compendium, 147, 150
Sultanate of Brunei, 119
Switzerland, three races in, 38
Sydney and federal tariff, 83

T

Taj, architecture of the, 31
Tasmania, 91; vote on Commonwealth Bill, 72

INDEX

Transvaal, 2
    Dutch-Afrikander State, 105
    Effect of gold discoveries in, 44
    Foreign element in, 106
Trinidad, 124
Tunis, 46

U

Uganda—
    And Foreign Office, 103
    Foreign Office Army in, 12
    Money spent on railroad to, 113
United Empire Loyalists, Canada, 33
"United Kingdom" excludes India and Crown Colonies, 136
United States—
    Military Service in, 43
    Territory and wealth, 4
United States and Canada—
    Comparison between, 34
    Trade between, 137, 138
United States and West Indies, 122, 124
    Reciprocity trade between, 137
Upper Canada, 40
Utrecht, Treaty of, and Newfoundland, 47, 56, 65

V

Versailles, Treaty of, and Newfoundland, 48

Victoria—
    Effect of gold discoveries in, 44
    Vote on Commonwealth Bill, 72, 83

W

Walker, Sir Baldwin, action in Newfoundland, 59
West Africa Frontier Force, 12
West Coast of Africa, four Crown Colonies, 101
West Indies—
    Government of, 15
    Negro Slavery in, 122
    Populations, 123
    Productions and trade, 121, 124
    Prospects of, 122, 126
    Sugar industry, 3, 121
West Indies and United States, reciprocity trade between, 137
Western Australia, attitude towards Commonwealth Bill, 80, 83
White Nile Sphere of Influence, 101
Wilkinson, Spencer, his books recommended, 146, 151

Z

Zambesi River, 100, 103, 106
Zanzibar, Sultan of, dominions, 101
Zollverein, proposals for, 140, 141

www.ingramcontent.com/pod-product-compliance
Lightning Source LLC
Chambersburg PA
CBHW020312170426
43202CB00008B/576